Life of Fred®

Classes

Life of Fred® Classes

Stanley F. Schmidt, Ph.D.

Polka Dot Publishing

ISBN: 978-1-937032-15-9

Printed and bound in the United States of America

Polka Dot Publishing   Reno, Nevada

To order copies of books in the Life of Fred series,

visit our website PolkaDotPublishing.com

Questions or comments? Email the author at lifeoffred@yahoo.com

Second printing

Life of Fred: Classes was illustrated by the author with additional clip art furnished under license
from Nova Development Corporation, which holds the copyright to that art.

for Goodness' sake

or as J.S. Bach—who was
never noted for his plain
English—often expressed it:

Ad Majorem Dei Gloriam
(to the greater glory of God)

If you happen to spot an error that the author, the publisher, and the printer missed, please let us know with an email to: lifeoffred@yahoo.com

SPECIAL
OFFER

As a reward, we'll email back to you a list of all the corrections that readers have reported.

A Note Before We Begin

This is the third language arts book in the Life of Fred® series. In these books, we will cover English from every angle.

In this third book you will learn:

★ the seven parts of speech
★ how you first learned what the word *dog* meant (hint: it wasn't from the dictionary.)
★ more of the continuing story of *Ducky Sings Opera*
★ four common errors in using adjectives
★ four uses of italics
★ how to determine if a verb is irregular
★ easy ways to tell if the tense is progressive or perfect or both
★ which adjectives don't have a comparative or a superlative form
★ how the present tense can exist outside of time
★ transitive verbs with direct and indirect objects
★ the nominative, possessive, and objective cases
★ what a simile is and the schwa in the word *simile*

. . . and that's only up to page 39!

HOW THIS BOOK IS ORGANIZED

Each chapter is a daily lesson. There are four pages of reading about the adventures of Fred and a Your Turn to Play.

Have a paper and pencil handy before you sit down to read.

Each Your Turn to Play consists of about three or four questions. Write out the answers—don't just orally answer them.

After all the questions are answered, then take a peek at my answers that are given on the next page.

<u>Don't just read the questions and look at the answers.</u> You won't learn as much that way.

This was in my father's collection of photographs. It made me think about how some things have changed . . . and some have not.

I bet the trees are larger now.

Back then, an important part of schooling was "readin', writin', and 'rithmetic."

Today English and mathematics remain at the heart of education.

The *Life of Fred* math series takes you up through two years of college calculus, a year of college statistics, and one upper-division math course.

In the four books of the *Life of Fred* language arts series, you will learn more English than 95% of American high school graduates know.

And, as a bonus, in this book you'll also learn about making minestrone soup.

Contents

Chapter One
The Central Meaning of Life

F red's second hour of teaching English in Australia began. It had been quite an adventure getting to this point. Fred was looking forward to his nine o'clock class.

The dozen sixth graders from his eight o'clock class decided to stay in the classroom for another hour. Fourteen eleventh graders came into the room.

It was starting to get a little crowded. There weren't enough chairs for everyone. Some of the eleventh graders sat on top of the desks. Some sat on the floor.

All of the jitters* that he had had an hour ago were gone. Fred was ready to teach the way he had taught at KITTENS University for years.

One important thing that a teacher can do is provide the overall picture of his subject so that the students don't get lost in all the details. ☆ In business, it's about succeeding financially.

---

* His *apprehensiveness* was gone. There wasn't the *anxiety* that he had felt before: no *unease*, no *disquietude*, no *trepidation*.

Do you remember how a **thesaurus** works? You look up an idea, and it will give you words.

☆ In math, everything revolves around numbers, shapes, and sets.

☆ In football, it's all about winning.

☆ In life, it all boils down to two choices: A) me, me, me or B) loving.

☆ In English . . . Fred wasn't sure. *How can you organize English?* Fred thought to himself.

Fred did what some teachers do when he can't figure out the answer. He asked his students. "Can anyone tell me how English is organized?"

Sixth grader Helen said, "That's easy. There are seven parts of speech."

Fred was thinking: *the tongue, the lips, the lungs*—but those aren't the parts of speech.

Helen continued, "As everyone knows, they are (1) nouns, (2) pronouns, (3) verbs, (4) conjunctions, (5) prepositions, (6) adjectives, and (7) adverbs. Every word in a sentence is one of these."

Time Out!

Some of these seven parts of speech we have looked at before.

✳ Nouns are persons, places, or things.

✳ Pronouns stand in place of nouns: I, we, you, he, she, it, they.

> ❋ Verbs are the action words in sentences.
>
> ❋ Conjunctions join two simple sentences together to prevent a run-on: and, but, or, after, although, as if, because, before, if, though, till, unless, when, where, and while. Betty washed the dishes while Alexander dried them.
>
> It would be a run-on to write: Betty washed the dishes, Alexander dried them.
>
> We have done four out of the seven.

Fred hadn't had a chance to read some books on language arts. (past perfect) Reading is often the fastest way to learn. But right now he needed to get through these Wednesday (silent *d*) classes. Then, he hoped he could get to the library or the bookstore and study in the evening.

He had to teach on the fly.*

Helen had said that every word in a sentence is one of the seven parts of speech. At this

What you get when you take an idiom literally

point Fred wasn't quite sure what prepositions, adjectives and adverbs were, but he was going to find out.

———————————————

* *On the fly* = something done without preparation. (an idiom)

Fred said, "Please turn to the second page in your textbook, *Ducky Sings Opera.*"

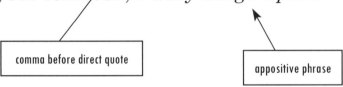

comma before direct quote		appositive phrase

(Fred had already done the first page with the eight o'clock class.)

The producer of the opera was overjoyed. A real Duck had applied for the role and not a man.

Fred started with the parts of speech that he knew. "Can anyone identify the nouns in these two sentences?"

Twenty-six students raised their hands. Peter copied the two sentences on the blackboard and circled the nouns.

The (producer) of the (opera) was overjoyed. A real (Duck) had applied for the (role) and not a (man.)

Nouns are persons, places, or things: car, Christina Rossetti, freedom, Kansas, music, pizza.

"Can anyone identify the verbs?"

Hans copied the two sentences on the blackboard and underlined the verbs.

The producer of the opera <u>was</u> overjoyed. A real Duck <u>had applied</u> for the role and not a man.

The conjunction was easy to find.

The producer of the opera was overjoyed. A real Duck had applied for the role (and) not a man.

There weren't any pronouns in those two sentences.

Your Turn to Play

The next sentence in the book was:
Ducky lost a feather in his excitement because jobs for tenors are hard to find.

1. List the nouns in that sentence.
2. List the verbs.
3. List the conjunction(s).
4. The only pronouns that we have mentioned so far are: *I, we, you, he, she, it,* and *they*.

   Each of these seven pronouns has three forms.

   For example, the three forms of *I* are *I, my,* and *me*.

With that hint, list the one pronoun in the Ducky sentence.

. . . . **ANSWERS** . . . .

Ducky lost a feather in his excitement because jobs for tenors are hard to find.

1. The nouns are Ducky, feather, excitement, jobs, and tenors.
2. The verbs are lost, are, and find.
3. The conjunction is because.
4. The pronoun is his.

Just for fun, the first three sentences of this chapter were written in different past tenses. *Tense* is the Latin word for *time.*

Fred's second hour of teaching English in Australia began. (Past tense.)

It had been quite an adventure getting to this point. (Past perfect tense. In the perfect tenses, the action stops.)

Fred was looking forward to his nine o'clock class.

(Past progressive tense. The "ing" on the verb emphasizes the action in progress.)

Chapter Two
Prepositions in 30 Seconds

F red was amazed at how much English these students already knew. He had a lot of catching up to do. Even the sixth graders were acquainted with the seven parts of speech. He still needed to learn about prepositions, adjectives, and adverbs.

"Let's play a game," Fred announced. "It's called Five Minute Teacher. You have five minutes to be the teacher and present everything you can about prepositions."

Twenty-six hands were eagerly raised. Fred pointed to Peter. He was a sixth grader, and he would be teaching both sixth graders and eleventh graders.

Peter began, "Prepositions."

Fred looked at the clock. Peter had four minutes and fifty-five seconds left.

Peter cleared his throat.

He had four minutes and fifty-two seconds left.

He rolled up his sleeve and pointed to a chart on the side wall.

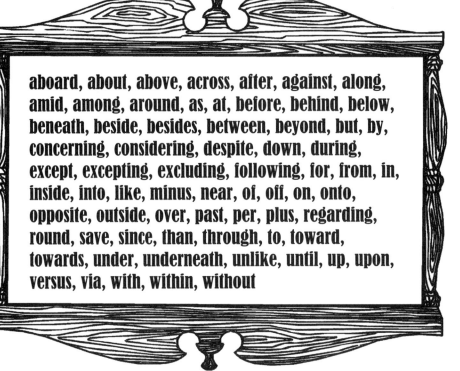

aboard, about, above, across, after, against, along, amid, among, around, as, at, before, behind, below, beneath, beside, besides, between, beyond, but, by, concerning, considering, despite, down, during, except, excepting, excluding, following, for, from, in, inside, into, like, minus, near, of, off, on, onto, opposite, outside, over, past, per, plus, regarding, round, save, since, than, through, to, toward, towards, under, underneath, unlike, until, up, upon, versus, via, with, within, without

Peter had four minutes and fifty seconds left. He began to hurry. "Prepositions are used in prepositional phrases. If we look at our *Ducky Sings Opera* textbook, we can spot prepositional phrases easily."

The eleven prepositional phrases are underlined.

In his excitement, Ducky ran outside his apartment with his loose feather underneath his wing. He looked behind the barn, near the water fountain, beside the river, but couldn't find any friends in the neighborhood except the crows who sat on the telephone wires above him.

He had four minutes and thirty seconds left. Peter sat down. He couldn't think of anything more to say about prepositions. The class applauded.

Fred asked, "Does anyone have anything that they would like to add to Peter's preposition presentation?" (alliteration = using the same sound at the beginning of several words)

Tom said, "Perhaps Peter might have pointed to the multi-word preposition poster pasted to the wall in my proximity." (Once you start doing alliteration it can be hard to stop.)

according to
because of
by way of
in addition to
in front of
in place of
in regard to
in spite of
instead of
on account of
out of

Up to this point, four sixth graders—Hans, Peter, Tom, and Helen—had done all the talking.

None of the 14 eleventh graders (was able/were able)* to get a word in.

Rosie, an eleventh grader, raised her hand. "Neither of these poster lists is

---

* This is a question in subject-verb agreement. The rule was to shrink down the extra garbage in the sentence: None of the 14 eleventh graders was able to get a word in.

None is the subject and it is singular. It is easy to get distracted by the plural: *the 14 eleventh graders*.

complete. (Not *are complete*.) The first poster doesn't have *till* or *unto*, and the second poster is missing *in view of, apart from,* and *up to.*"

Peter responded, "I agree. Neither the first poster nor the second poster (list/lists) all the prepositions.* They offer only samples."

Fred now knew five of the seven parts of speech: nouns, pronouns, verbs, conjunctions, and prepositions. All that were left were adjectives and adverbs. Adjectives are easy and adverbs aren't that hard.

---

* The rules for *or* or *nor*:

    If both subjects are singular, then the verb is singular.**

        Neither the first poster nor the second poster lists all the prepositions.

    If either (or both) subjects are plural, the verb agrees with the subject closest to it.

        Pie and pizzas are my favorite foods.

        Thursdays or Fridays are fine with me.

        The states or the federal government is the choice.

** Is it possible to have a footnote to a footnote? I'm not sure. In any event, I've got to point out that the singular verb can have an *s*, such as in *He sits.* The corresponding plural verb doesn't have an *s*, such as in *They sit.*

    This is just the opposite of nouns: *one bird, two birds.*

Your Turn to Play

1. The list of prepositions was given three pages ago. Create a sentence about eating pizza (or whatever your favorite food is) that contains five prepositional phrases.

2. Proofread this next part of the *Ducky Sings Opera* story.   Two errors in each paragraph.

Ducky wanted to tell his friends that he often called his feather friends that he had recieved a job offer.

He ran in his house and turned on his computer. The screen remained black. He knew that either the monitor or the connections was bad.

. . . .**ANSWERS** . . . .

1.   *Near dawn, unlike many others in my family, I, despite the darkness, lay beneath the covers of my bed considering the toppings of the pizza from the giant list of toppings on the posters on the walls of my room that I would use in the creation of the world's best pizza excluding the seven creations I had made in the previous week.*

My sentence has more than five prepositional phrases. I was having too much fun.

Near dawn,
unlike many others
in my family, I,
despite the darkness, lay
beneath the covers
of my bed considering the toppings

of the pizza
from the giant list
of toppings
on the posters
on the walls
of my room that I would use
in the creation
of the world's best pizza
excluding the seven creations I had made
in the previous week.

his friends, which he often called his
feather friends, that he
that/which error
The phrase *he often called his feather friends*
is an add-on. Removing it does not change
the real meaning of the sentence.

Ducky wanted to tell his friends that he often called his
feather friends that he had recieved a job offer.

into
If he were running
around on a track
inside of his house,
then you could say he
was running in his
house.

received
The old rule: *i before e, except
after c*

He ran in his house and turned on his computer. The
screen remained black. He knew that either the monitor
or the connections was bad.

were
The subject (connections)
closest to the verb is plural

Chapter Three
Teaching by Giving Examples

Fred was having a pleasant time teaching in an Australian classroom. The difficult job of conjugating a verb in twelve tenses has already been done. The easy task of learning what an adjective is lay ahead of him.

(The adjectives in the previous paragraph are in a gray font.)

Wait a minute! I, your reader, object. If you are going to explain what an adjective is, shouldn't you first define it before giving examples? You have everything backwards. That's bad teaching.

Hold it. Did you just put one of my precious words in a gray font? You are making me crazy.

Teaching by first giving examples is a very natural way to learn new things. Do you remember when you were a little kid and your older sister was teaching you how to talk?

Suppose you had one of these in your home, and your sister wanted to teach you the word *dog*. She would point to the dog and say, "Dog." She would teach you by example. She didn't start by giving

you the official definition first: A dog is a carnivorous four-legged mammal, *Canis familiaris,* that likes to bark at night.

     Examples of adjectives:
         the warm evening
         a delicious, gooey pizza
         they were happy
         a friendly puppy
         the prom dress was red

Adjectives sharpen the meaning of a noun. It was not just a dress. It was a prom dress, and it was red.

Fred said to his class, "Using adjectives is an important part of good writing. There are three major mistakes that beginning writers make.

"The first mistake is using unnecessary adjectives. Let's look at the next page of *Ducky Sings Opera*."
Ducky's electric computer wasn't working. Even after he kicked it, the non-functioning computer didn't make an audible sound.

What other kind of computer is there?   We already said it wasn't working.
               Unnecessary.

"The second mistake is in using weak adjectives. If everything is *wonderful*, then the word loses its meaning."

Rosie raised her hand. "The best example I have ever encountered of a weak adjective was when my older sister went on a three-week vacation with her husband to Hawaii where they went swimming every morning in the warm ocean, toured the pineapple and orchid plantations, and dined out under the stars every evening.

"When I asked her how her vacation was, she answered, 'It was nice.'

"*Nice* was a very weak adjective."

Time Out!

When a quotation extends for more than one paragraph, you start each paragraph with an open quotes ("), but put the close quotes only at the end of the last paragraph (").

To understand what this means, please look at Fred's two-paragraph quote on the previous page and Rosie's three-paragraph quote on this page.

Second Time Out!

In Rosie's second paragraph, she had a quote inside of a quote. The inside quote uses only single quote marks (' ').

"The other error in using adjectives," Fred continued, "is in overusing them. Whoever wrote *Ducky** went overboard (an idiom) in this next passage."

Ducky's flat, yellow, webbed foot was painful, smarting, throbbing, agonizing, and intolerable, because he had hit his foot against his hard, unyielding, adamant computer.

"You can always tell when a writer has just bought a new thesaurus."

Rosie wrote in her class notes:

There are three kinds of adjectival errors:
1. unnecessary adjectives —briny ocean
2. weak adjectives —the hurricane was unpleasant
3. too many adjectives —my true, real, honest love

---

* Sometimes book titles are referred to by just one word of the title.

When Fred saw her notes, he smiled when he saw the word *adjectival*. (ag-ik-TIE-vəl where ə is a schwa—the reduced vowel sound like the *i* in easily)

The word *adjective* is a noun. It is a part of speech. If you turn *adjective* into an adjective, it becomes the word *adjectival*.

In short, *adjectival* is the adjectival form of *adjective*!

Your Turn to Play

1. If you turned the word *noun* into a noun, how would it be spelled?

2. Fill in one word: An _____ is a part of speech used to sharpen the meaning of a noun.

3. (harder question) Those things mentioned in the previous question* modify not only nouns but one other part of speech. Name that other part of speech that they can modify. Is it pronouns, verbs, conjunctions, prepositions, adjectives, or adverbs?

---

* I don't want to say *adjectives* because I don't want to give away the answer to the previous question.

```
...... ANSWERS .......
```

1. This is too easy. The word *noun* is already a noun.
It is spelled n-o-u-n.

2. An _adjective_ is a part of speech used to sharpen
the meaning of a noun.

3. Do you remember when I was giving examples of
adjectives? One example was: they were happy.

   Adjectives modify either nouns or pronouns.

Italics are used for several purposes.

You have seen them used for book titles,
such as *Moby Dick*.

They can be used to *really emphasize*
something.

The third use of italics is when we are
looking at a word as a word, rather than what
the word means.

✓ Red is a color. *Red* has three letters.

✓ *Adjectival* is the adjectival form of *adjective*.

They can also be used for foreign words
such as *Canis familiaris* (Latin) or the
Norwegian idiom: *Han er darlig utstyrt i oeverst
etasje.*

Chapter Four
A Piece of Cake

Fred felt very good about teaching English. This was his first day of teaching and by the time he had gotten half way through his second class, he had covered six of the seven parts of speech.

He said, "Now that we have covered six of the seven parts of speech. . . ."

The class broke into laughter. They thought he was trying to be funny.

Fred thought:

✳ *Are there more than seven parts of speech?*

✳ *Is my hair standing up?*

✳ *Did someone draw a funny picture?*

Rosie said, "You are so silly. (present tense) We know you are just kidding." (present progressive)

Fred didn't know what to say. (past tense) He hadn't been kidding. (past perfect progressive—something begun in the past and then stopped.)

Fred told the truth, "But I wasn't kidding. (past progressive) I'm confused. Please help me. What was funny."

Tom said, "You said that you had covered the six of the seven parts of speech."

Fred nodded.

"Were you serious when you said you covered nouns, pronouns, verbs, conjunctions, prepositions, and adjectives?"

Fred answered in a very weak voice, "I thought we said everything that could be said about those six topics. You mean there's more to be said?"

The 26 students all nodded their heads.

Fred looked at the clock and felt relieved. He knew that tonight he would find every English book that he could and he would learn why the students had laughed (past perfect) at him when he said (past tense) that he had covered six of the seven parts of speech.

The sixth graders and the eleventh graders did not leave the room. They wanted to stay for another hour of instruction.

There were 26 students in the classroom right now. Fred wondered who would be the students for his ten o'clock class.

Everyone waited. No one came. Then Rosie said, "I bet I know where Suzie is. She often gets distracted and forgets to come to class."

Rosie, Fred, and the other 25 students all headed outside. Suzie was playing and wasn't aware that it was time for class.

Rosie told Suzie, "It's time to come inside for class."

Fred was very happy that Suzie left her animal outside.

Suzie sat in a chair directly in front of Fred while the other 26 students formed a semicircle around her. They were going to watch Fred teach Suzie. They didn't tell Fred that Suzie is not some uneducated little kid. (litotes)

Fred wrote on the blackboard: ABCDEFGHIJKLMNOPQRSTUVWXYZ. He thought that would be a good place to start. Suzie looked bored.

He thought that he might be going too fast for his little student. He switched to something

easier, "Do you know what *color* means?" He
held up a fistful of crayons.

Suzie frowned. "Do you mean what part of
speech is the word *color*? That's a tricky
question. I'm glad you're not treating me like a
baby. *Color* is, of course, a noun—as in the
sentence: Blue is a color.

"And *color* is a transitive verb—as in: I will
color the wall with orange paint. *Wall* is the
object of the verb *color*.

"And *color* can be used as an adjective—as
in my color television."

Fred colored. He realized that this could
be a very long classroom hour.

"Oh, you reminded me," she continued. "To
color can be an intransitive verb, which means
to blush as you are doing right now."

Social note

If you point out to someone that they are blushing, that
can make them even more embarrassed. Fred turned from a
light pink into a dark pink.

Suzie added, "*Color* is a regular verb. In
the present tense, third person singular, it is he
colors. In the past tense, he colored. In the past
perfect, he had colored."

Fred knew how he could find out how much Suzie knew. He asked her to conjugate the irregular verb *to go*. Instead of doing all three persons in both the singular and the plural, Fred asked that she just do the third person singular. She said that was as easy as pie.* Suzie wrote the 12 tenses on the board.

Conjugation of to go in the third person singular

Present tense	he goes
Past tense	he went
Future tense	he will go
Present progressive	he is going
Past progressive	he was going
Future progressive	he will be going
Present perfect	he has gone
Past perfect	he had gone
Future perfect	he will have gone
Present perfect progressive	he has been going
Past perfect progressive	he had been going
Future perfect progressive	he will have been going

Your Turn to Play Do this for the verb *to fly*. Do not look at the next page until you have done all the work on paper first.

---

* *As easy as pie* is an idiom = something that is simple and pleasurable. It has nothing to do with the number pi ($\pi \doteq 3.14159$) or with making a pie. It is a shortened form of *as easy as eating pie*. It means the same thing as the idiom *a piece of cake*.

> **. . . . . . . ANSWER . . . .**
>
> Present tense   he flies
> Past tense   he flew
> Future tense   he will fly
>
> Present progressive   he is flying
> Past progressive   he was flying
> Future progressive   he will be flying
>
> Present perfect   he has flown
> Past perfect   he had flown
> Future perfect   he will have flown
>
> Present perfect progressive   he has been flying
> Past perfect progressive   he had been flying
> Future perfect progressive   he will have been flying

Let's just look at the future perfect for a moment: *He will have flown.*

The perfect tense indicates that there is an action that is stopped.

The sentence might read: *He will have flown for six hours before he lands.*

Chapter Five
Simplifying the Tenses

Fred's head was spinning a little with the twelve tenses. He thought *There must be some way to simplify that mess.* He looked at what Suzie had written on the board:

Present tense	he goes
Past tense	he went
Future tense	he will go
Present progressive	he is going
Past progressive	he was going
Future progressive	he will be going
Present perfect	he has gone
Past perfect	he had gone
Future perfect	he will have gone
Present perfect progressive	he has been going
Past perfect progressive	he had been going
Future perfect progressive	he will have been going

and suddenly it all made sense.

Question: How do you tell if you are using one of the six progressive tenses? (If you just look at the chart for a moment, it will be clear.)

Answer: The verb has an *-ing* tacked on the end.

Suzie was quick to point out, "Of course, if the verb has *ing* to start with, then the progressive form has an extra *ing*. Look at the verb *ring*." She headed to the board and wrote:

Present tense	it rings
Past tense	it rang
Future tense	it will ring
Present progressive	it is ringing
Past progressive	it was ringing
Future progressive	it will be ringing
Present perfect	it has rung
Past perfect	it had rung
Future perfect	it will have rung
Present perfect progressive	it has been ringing
Past perfect progressive	it had been ringing
Future perfect progressive	it will have been ringing

Question: How do you tell if you are using one of the six perfect tenses?   (If you just look at the chart for a moment, it will be clear.)

Answer: Each of the perfect tenses contains *has, had, or have.*

Using a little alliteration, Suzie said, "And as a <u>b</u>onus, you use <u>*been*</u> when you have <u>b</u>oth <u>p</u>erfect and <u>p</u>rogressive."

Fred thought *Verbs are certainly not the simplest part of speech. What about adjectives? There couldn't be anything messy about them.* He took a chance and said, "Adjectives."

Suzie's eyes lit up.

She said, "Adjectives are words that modify nouns or pronouns."

Fred was relieved. She was keeping it easy.

"As everyone knows," she continued, "adjectives come in three forms: the positive, the comparative, and the superlative." (sue-PURR-lə-tive, where ə is a schwa like the u in circus)

Suzie went to the blackboard. Fred went and sat in Suzie's chair.

She wrote:

Positive	Comparative	Superlative
hard	harder	hardest
quick	quicker	quickest
dry	drier	driest
long	longer	longest

Fred thought of an old saying, "*Good, better, best. You never let it rest, till good is better, and better is best.*"

Suzie pretended like she was the teacher. She asked Fred, "What are the comparative and superlative forms of the adjective *smooth*?"

Fred smiled. He knew the answer, "The comparative and superlative forms are *smoother* and *smoothest*."

Suzie asked, "And what are the comparative and superlative forms of the adjective *talkative?*"

Without thinking, he responded, "*Talkativer* and *talkativest*." Fred colored and corrected himself, "*More talkative* and *most talkative*."

Suzie continued, "The positive, comparative and superlative forms of some adjectives are not as simple as *small, smaller,* and *smallest*.

"To conclude my lecture on adjectives. . . ."

Fred couldn't believe his ears. He thought *This little kid doesn't sound like a little kid.*

". . . I will discuss the two ways that nouns or verbs are turned into adjectives. The first way to turn nouns into adjectives uses proper nouns.* Texas oil wells
Washington University
a Paris art show
United States colonies

---

* Proper nouns are names of people, places, or institutions. They are capitalized.

"The second way is to add a **suffix*** to nouns or verbs. The most common suffixes are: *–able, –ed, –ful, –less,* and *–y.*"

    to do → doable

    sugar → sugared

    to forget → forgetful

    to fear → fearless

    dream → dreamy

Your Turn to Play

1. Name two more nouns or verbs that can be turned into adjectives using the suffixes *–able, –ed, –ful, –less,* or *–y.*

2. In which of the twelve tenses is the verb:

    2A) *I am going to sneeze.*

    2B) *I had been blowing my nose all during allergy season.*

    2C) *You supplied me with six handkerchiefs.*

3. (harder question) *Unique* is an adjective. Fred has a unique nose. What is the comparative and superlative forms of *unique*?

---

* Suffixes are added to the ends of words. Prefixes are added to the beginning of words.

. . . . . . .ANSWERS . . . .

1. There are many possible answers. Your answers will probably be different than mine.

    to teach → teachable

      fruit → fruited

        duty → dutiful

          to dream → dreamless

            cream → creamy

2A) *I am going to sneeze.*

The *–ing* on the verb indicates a progressive tense. If it were the past progressive, it would have been: I was going to sneeze. Future progressive: I will be going to sneeze. *I am going to sneeze* is the present progressive.

2B) *I had been blowing my nose all during allergy season.* The word *been* automatically indicates both perfect and progressive. This sentence is in the past perfect progressive.

2C) *You supplied me with six handkerchiefs.* A simple past tense.

3. *Unique* means the one and only, there is no other. It's nonsense to talk about one thing being "more unique" than another.

    "More unique" is in scare quotes. Scare quotes are used by writers to indicate that they don't believe what's inside the quotes. E.g., Social Security "contribution." (Contributions are supposed to be voluntary.)

Chapter Six
Hoppy

S uzie wanted to go outside and play. She had been playing the role of teacher, so she announced, "It's time for a field trip. Everyone follow me."

The 12 sixth graders, the 14 eleventh graders, and Fred followed Suzie. Fred didn't know what to expect. She was a very exceptional child.

She continued her lecture. "This is my friend Hoppy. Together, Hoppy and I* make a terrific teaching team. (alliteration) I will say a sentence and the 27 of you tell me everything you can about the sentence.

"My first sentence is *I like Hoppy*."

Helen said, "It is in the present tense."

Tom: "The subject is first person singular."

---

* You don't say, "Hoppy and me make a terrific teaching team." *Hoppy* and *I* are the subjects of the sentence. *Me* can't be the subject of a sentence. You don't say, "Me is going to the store."

Peter: "*Like* is a transitive verb. The object is *Hoppy*."

All these comments were old stuff. Rosie added something new, "The present tense is often used in English to say something that is always true. The present tense can exist outside of time. When you say, 'I like Hoppy,' you mean that you like Hoppy right now, you liked Hoppy yesterday, and you will like Hoppy next week. Each of these sentences has the present, the past, and the future all wrapped up in them:

> A square has four sides.
>
> The earth is round.
>
> God is love.
>
> *Pizza* is spelled with two z's."

Suzie continued, "My second sentence is *I gave Hoppy a hug*."

Peter said, "*Gave* is a transitive verb. I can't figure out what the object is."

Suzie asked, "Did I give Hoppys* or did I give hugs?"

---

*Chapter 11 of *Life of Fred: Begin Teaching* listed 16 ways to make plurals. The 15th way dealt with people's names.

"You gave hugs," Peter said.

Suzie smiled and said, "So *a hug* is the **direct object** of *gave* in the sentence *I gave Hoppy a hug*."

This is Hoppy.

"But, but, but, what is Hoppy?" Hans asked.

Suzie pointed to Hoppy.

"No. What I meant is if *hug* is the direct object in the sentence *I gave Hoppy a hug*, then what do you call *Hoppy* in that sentence?"

"Hoppy is the **indirect object**," Suzie explained. "Indirect objects are pretty rare. They only come with verbs like *ask, tell,* or *give*."

Helen said, "I thought that there were only seven parts of speech: nouns, pronouns, verbs, conjunctions, prepositions, adjectives, and adverbs. Are direct objects and indirect objects the eighth and ninth parts of speech?"

Rosa said, "No. There may be more and more ways to make plurals in English, but the number of parts of speech will remain at seven."

She held up her copy of *Ducky Sings Opera*, which every student carried, and read the next sentence in the story: After Ducky had hit his foot against the computer, he gave the computer one minute to turn on.

Rosa said, "The direct object is *minute*. The indirect object is *computer*. Both of these are nouns. So direct and indirect objects are always nouns. We still have seven parts of speech."

Tom cleared his throat and quietly asked, "What about the next sentence in the story? After one minute, Ducky gave it a whack with his baseball bat."

Rosa said, "You're right. The indirect object is *it*. So direct and indirect objects can be either nouns or pronouns."

Suzie nodded. She liked it when her students discovered things without having to be told.*

---

* Often, the least effective way to teach something is to lecture. If Suzie had just said that direct and indirect objects are nouns or pronouns, many of her students would not remember that. Instead, when Helen, Rosa, and Tom figured that out, it might have made much more of a lasting impression.

   In math, when students *discover* that if you connect the midpoints of any four-sided figure, you will always get a parallelogram (opposite sides are parallel) they will remember it a lot longer than if you just tell them.

Your Turn to Play

1. Make up three sentences that have both direct and indirect objects in them.

   In the first sentence use the verb *offered*. In the second sentence, *asked*. In the third sentence, *mailed*.

2. Make up a sentence in the present tense that is always true.

3. Make up a sentence in the present tense that is sometimes true and sometimes false.

4. The positive, comparative, and superlative forms of the adjective *wet* are *wet*, *wetter*, and *wettest*.

Give the three forms of *loud*.

Give the three forms of *perfect*.

· · · · · · ·**ANSWERS**· · · · · · ·

1. My sentences will probably be different than yours.
    She offered her mule a carnation.
    She asked her mule a question about calculus.
    She mailed her brother the mule.

2. My sentences will probably be different than yours.
    Humans eat food.
    A triangle has three sides.
    Inflammable things are flammable.

3. Birds fly. (Some birds cannot fly.)
    The sky is blue.
    Teenagers make good choices.

4. loud, louder, loudest

    The adjective *perfect* is like the adjective *unique*.
You can't get more perfect than perfect.

Chapter Seven
Cases

uzie gave Hoppy a pat on his head. Hoppy hopped into the woods, and she ran after him. The sixth graders and the eleventh graders knew that Fred's ten o'clock class was over. Everyone left. It was 10:30.

Fred was standing alone on the lawn. It would be a half hour before his eleven o'clock class.

He thought about the sentence:

Suzie gave Hoppy a pat on his head.
subject   verb   indirect object direct object prepositional phrase

He knew that subjects and objects can be either nouns or pronouns.

She gave him a pat on his head.
pronoun   pronoun   noun

He giggled and changed the pronouns:
Her gave he a pat on him head.

That sounded really dumb.

Pronouns have several forms: I, me, my. Which one you use depends on *where in the sentence* they are. You don't say, "Me likes ice cream."

There are three different places nouns and pronouns can be in a sentence. They don't call them *places* in a sentence; that would make it too easy.

Instead, they call them **cases**.

The **nominative case** is the subject of the sentence. I, we, you, he, she, it, they, and who. (Who is also a pronoun.)

The **objective case** is direct and indirect objects and in prepositional phrases. Me, us, you, him, her, it, them, and whom.

The **possessive case** shows ownership. My, our, your, his, her, its, their, and whose.

In the *Ducky* story, the most recent (superlative form of the adjective) sentence was:

After one minute, Ducky gave it a whack with his baseball bat.

objective case   nominative case   objective case   objective case   possessive case

So verbs have tenses.
Nouns and pronouns have cases.
Nouns have (16) plurals.
Adjectives have forms.   (positive, comparative, and superlative)
And the North Pole has snow.

Time Out for Older Readers!

Fred wondered what he had gotten himself into. **(past perfect)** For five years he had taught mathematics at KITTENS University. Math seemed so straightforward. If you have a division of fractions, $\frac{1}{2} \div \frac{2}{5}$, you changed it into a multiplication problem, $\frac{1}{2} \times \frac{5}{2}$

The hardest part of algebra was teaching "word problems," and that was because it involved English. Once the English got translated into an equation, it was smooth sailing. **(idiom)**

Math seemed to him like a diamond. It was stable and unchanging. English seemed like a ripe tomato.*

Fred didn't have much problem with the nominative case. Subjects are in the nominative case.

The objective case is also called the accusative case. Direct and indirect objects and nouns or pronouns in prepositional phrases are in the accusative case.

The possessive case is also called the genitive case.

Now things get **really deep** . . .

---

* *Like a ripe tomato* is a **simile** (SIM-ə-lee, where ə is a schwa like the *e* in system.)

Similes can make your writing more alive. If you write that English is soft and subject to decay, few readers will remember your words.

When you learn that *schwa* can also be spelled *shwa,* you might start to think that English seems like holding a small octopus in your hand. English squirms. It changes shape.

English isn't all bad. It's better than math for telling people that you care for them.

But an octopus in your hand can also be a good thing . . . if you're really hungry.

really deep
Time Out for Really Old Readers!

Item #1: The pronouns in the possessive (genitive) case are my, our, your, his, her, its, their, and whose.

There are seven parts of speech: nouns, pronouns, verbs, conjunctions, prepositions, adjectives, and adverbs.

When you write, "His hat is green," is *his* a pronoun or is it an adjective?

Item #2: There are two forms of the possessive (genitive) pronouns! If the pronoun goes directly in front of the noun, we have: *my* dog, *our* dog, *your* dog, *her* dog, *their* dog.

Otherwise, we have:

The dog is *mine/ours/yours/hers/theirs.*[*]

To make things a little more complicated, *his* and *its* do not have two different forms.

Item #3: English is hard when compared with math, but it is easy when compared to German. Our pronouns come in lots of cases, but our nouns have only two forms: *Helen* and *Helen's.*

In German, they add a fourth case: the dative case. Indirect objects are in the dative case. The German words for *the* and *a* change depending on which case the noun is in (and which gender the noun is).

In Latin, there is a fifth case: the ablative.

---

[*] Some people say that *my* is a possessive adjective and *mine* is a possessive pronoun.

His car = possessive adjective.

The car is *his* = possessive pronoun.

Your Turn to Play

1. Similes are fun. And they are not complicated.
Christina Rossetti wrote in *A Birthday*:

>   My heart is like an apple-tree
>   Whose boughs are bent with thickset fruit;
>   My heart is like a rainbow shell
>   That paddles in a halcyon sea;
>   My heart is gladder than all these
>   Because my love is come to me.

✻ halcyon (HAL-see-ən) = calm, happy, peaceful, carefree

✻ In most poetry the first word of each line is capitalized.

✻ Christina Rossetti was one of the most popular English poets of the 1800s.

Write a simile about your favorite song, food, or friend.

    My _____ is like _____.

2. The next sentence in *Ducky* is:
Ducky put his computer into the garbage can.

   Name the case of each noun and pronoun in that
sentence.

3. Ducky noticed that he had not plugged in the
computer. What tense is *had not plugged*?

4. He apologized to his computer. He walked outside.
The sky was blue. He thought that this was ideal weather
for ducks.

Give the positive, comparative, and superlative forms
of the adjectives *blue* and *ideal*.

. . . . ANSWERS . . . .

1. My answer will probably be different than yours.

My pizza is like the first days of spring.

My pizza is like a bouquet. bouquet (BOO-kay) = flowers in a bunch. It is *not* pronounced BOW-kay.

My pizza is like a playground for my mouth.

2. Ducky put his computer into the garbage can.
    nominative   possessive objective   objective

   In this sentence, *garbage* is an adjective. In English nouns can often be used as adjectives: the *metal* bell, the *school* book, the *Puritan* faith.

   And for variety, adjectives (if you put *a* or *the* in front of them) can be used as subjects in a sentence: The *idle* often do not have much joy. The *cool* of the evening is often most pleasant.

3. Ducky noticed that he had not plugged in the computer. This is in the past perfect. Before the *noticed* occurred, the *had not plugged* had happened.

The **auxiliary verbs** (helping verbs) *has, have,* and *had* are used in the perfect tenses.

4. blue (positive)

    bluer (comparative)   My sky is bluer than yours.

    bluest (superlative)

Ideal means something that can't be improved. Like *perfect* and *unique*, it does not have comparative or superlative forms.

Chapter Eight
Gray Skies

Fred was standing alone on the lawn in front of Dubbo School of English.

In the daytime the walls looked very bright. Fred was very happy to be teaching English here in Australia. He was delighted with how much the students already knew and how eager they were to participate.

He looked at the gray sky. He had learned that seasons are reversed below the equator, so a gray sky was not surprising. June in Australia might be a little like (June + six months) December in Kansas.

There was one difference that Fred noticed.* The air smelled funny.

---

* Not *which* Fred noticed. *That Fred noticed* is essential to the meaning of the sentence. We use *which* when the phrase is not essential to the rest of the sentence. For example, *The sky, which reminded Fred of Kansas, was gray.*

In fact, the air smelled really bad. It was like sitting next to someone who was smoking.[*]

Suzie and Hoppy came out of the woods. She pointed. Fred thought that she was pointing at him, but she wasn't.

She was pointing at Fred's house, which was behind Fred.

Fred turned around. His Gauss House was burning up.

Five things went through Fred's mind.
#1: My house is burning up . . . or is it burning down?

---

[*] When I was a college student back in the 1960s, students were allowed to smoke in the classrooms at my school. It was really bad when students on both sides of me would light up.

It was a balancing of two freedoms: Their freedom to smoke whenever they felt like it and my freedom to breathe clean air.

#2: Do I have any stuff in the house? No. No bow ties or math books. (This is a sentence fragment. These are Fred's thoughts. Usually, the sentence would be completed with . . . *are in that house.*)

#3: Is there any danger that the fire is going to spread to the school building? Not really. (Another sentence fragment.) *They are far enough apart.*

#4: Has anyone called the fire department?

Apparently, someone had.*

---

* This is an example of an **elliptical construction**. In formal English, no words are omitted: *Apparently, someone had called the fire department.*

There are four varieties of English: formal, informal, nonstandard, and general.

◆ Formal English has limited use: academic writing, science reports, lectures to special audiences. There are no elliptical constructions. In formal English: *I am taller than you are.* Not, *I am taller than you.*

◆ Informal English is used by educated people when talking with friends. It uses slang: *I made a boo-boo when I was at the mike.* Not, *I made a mistake when I was speaking at the microphone.*

◆ Nonstandard English. *You was. It don't make no never mind.*

◆ General English is the one to use 99% of the time. Most of the *Life of Fred* books are written in general English.

#5: *I'm homeless! Where can I sleep tonight? I wish I were back in Kansas.*

small essay

Two Ways Our Brains Work

We have two different types of thought: intellectual and emotional.

The intellectual part of brain work is calling figuring, learning, or cogitating. When Fred wondered whether the fire department had been called, he was doing this kind of thinking. In his math class, when he takes x + 3 = 8 and subtracts 3 from both sides and gets x = 5, it is a pure intellectual task.

When Fred thought *I'm homeless!* he was using the emotional side of his brain. He was starting to panic. Some psychologists say there are four basic emotions: glad, sad, mad, and afraid.

Be thankful that you have both kinds of thinking. If you only did intellectual thought, you might get a lot done, but you would miss out on really living. You would be like a cold calculator, incapable of loving or being loved.

Live a purely emotional life and you would get nothing accomplished. It is pretty easy to do—just take drugs that can turn your brain into cotton candy. Then you can sit in a corner and drool. You will see all kinds of pretty pictures in your head and hear spooky music, but you might be unable to go to the bathroom without someone else helping you.

It's the combination of intellectual and emotional thinking that makes life rich. The dancer's intellectual work of learning and practicing is driven by the thrill of performance. The mother spends years being a good mom because of the emotional rewards of seeing her kids develop into happy adults. The mathematician learns about taking the union of two sets—{⊠, ✈} ∪ {✈, 5} = {⊠, ✈, 5}—to later experience the joy of understanding why there are sets that are infinitely larger than {1, 2, 3, 4, . . .}. It is emotion that drives the intellectual side. Together they make sweet music.

end of small essay

Your Turn to Play

1. Insert *that* or *which*.

   Houses _____ are made of concrete don't burn down.

   Fred's pets _____ include cats, dogs, and llamas have been a source of anxiety to Kingie.

2. Ducky wanted to do the intelligent thing, so he decided to buy a new computer to replace his dead one.
   Give the positive, comparative, and superlative forms of the adjectives *intelligent* and *dead*.

3. (A harder question that few readers will get right)
   This is general English: Ducky wanted to do the intelligent thing, so he decided to buy a new computer to replace his dead one.

   It contains an elliptical construction. There is a word missing that would be inserted if this were formal English. What word?

   (*What word?* is also an elliptical construction. In formal English, it might be expressed as: *What word is missing?*)

. . . . ANSWERS . . . .

1.   Houses that are made of concrete don't burn down.

The phrase *that are made of concrete* is essential to the meaning of the sentence. If you omitted that phrase, the sentence, which once was true, would now be false.

Fred's pets, which include cats, dogs, and llamas, have been a source of anxiety to Kingie.

The meaning of the sentence doesn't change if you take out the phrase. *Which include cats, dogs, and llamas* just includes extra information.

Phrases beginning with *which* are set off from the rest of the sentence with commas.

2. intelligent (positive)
   more intelligent (comparative)
   most intelligent (superlative)

Dead is a word like *perfect, unique,* and *ideal* that does not have comparative or superlative forms.

3. Ducky wanted to do the intelligent thing, and so he decided to buy a new computer to replace his dead one.

or even more formally

Ducky wanted to do the intelligent thing, and therefore he decided to buy a new computer to replace his dead one.

Chapter Nine
A Place to Stay

Fred watched his Gauss House burn.

small essay
Our Inner Life

You can guess whether the intellectual question—Is my house burning up or burning down?—or the emotional thought—I'm homeless!—was uppermost in Fred's mind.

Emotion trumps reason.

Emotion beats reason.

Emotion smothers reason.

Emotion wins.

What things do you remember in your life? Most often you remember the emotional moments.

You remember birthday parties. (glad)

You remember your pet dying. (sad)

You remember times you were angry. (mad)

You remember times when you were a little kid at night and imagined some green-eyed gorilla hiding in your closet. (afraid)

If you are in an algebra class
and the teacher writes on the board $\quad 2x + 3x + 17 = 82$
and then combines the like terms $\qquad 5x + 17 = 82$
and then subtracts 17 from both sides $\qquad\qquad 5x = 65$
and then divides both sides by 5, $\qquad\qquad\qquad x = 13$

one key to your remembering all those steps is to tie the algebra to your emotions. And almost any emotion will work!

You might think, "This stuff will allow me to go to college" or "Learning this stuff will make my parents proud." (glad)

You might think, "I'm sorry that my parents never got a chance to learn this algebra." (sad)

You might think, "They won't be able to call me a dummy anymore. I'll show them." (mad)

The only emotion that doesn't work as well as the others is fear.

end of small essay

And Fred was feeling fear. He just stood there watching the flames.

He felt a hand on his shoulder.

Margie

It was the woman who had been nice to him on the first night he was at Dubbo. He had slept on her couch at her child protective services office.

She said, "I knew that I might find you here. Last night you told me, 'In the house right next to the Dubbo School of English—that's where I'm living this summer before I head back to Kansas in the fall.'

"It looks like you'll need a place to stay tonight," she continued.

Fred nodded. He could hardly talk. He was getting over the emotion of fear. Fear can FREEZE UP the brain. When a person is totally afraid, he can't even tell you what his name is.

She took his hand and they walked back to her car. As they walked, she told Fred that she had located "a very nice family" that he could stay with.

The word *nice* rattled around in Fred's head. It reminded him of real estate agents who talk about *lovely* homes and of people who talk about *fine* wines. These words are overused and have lost much of their exact meaning. All that is left is a general sense of approval. These are called **counterwords**.

These words are so general that they have little place in good writing.

Nice, before it was overused, used to mean "subtle or precise." An artist might have a nice sense of color, meaning a delicate perception of which colors to use. A writer might show a nice distinction by which words are used. The writer isn't just taking ideas and throwing words at it.

Margie said "a nice family" to Fred because she thought that he was only three years old and could only understand baby talk.

Fred asked, "What obligations will I incur in residing with them? I'm afraid that I could not compensate them monetarily given my current destitution."

Margie had been ready to give her usual speech to little kids. (past perfect tense) She was going to tell Fred that he would be living in nice house, that he would have nice food, and sleep in a nice bed. (was going = past progressive)

Instead, she responded, "You don't have to pay them. They are happy to provide you with a temporary place to stay."

"I certainly appreciate their beneficence.*"

As Fred climbed** into her car, she said that she was going to call them and tell them that they were coming.

As they drove, he fell asleep. This had been a long day so far. He had started the day at five minutes after three, had done proofreading at the local newspaper, had taken a nap at Gauss House, and had taught English for two and a half hours. Doing new things takes a lot more energy than doing the routine things. The first time you drive a car is usually much more

---

* bə-NEF-ə-səns where ə is pronounced like the *o* in gallop.
To be beneficent is to be good or charitable.

** Given Fred's size, *climbed* is probably a more accurate verb than *got into*.

demanding than the thousandth time you drive to work as an adult.

Fred had completely forgotten about the other classes he was supposed to teach that day. Emotional events ("I'm homeless!") can wipe out intellectual thoughts ("I've got a class at eleven").

Your Turn to Play

1. *Awful* is a counterword. It used to mean something that would inspire awe. Awe was an overwhelming feeling of admiration or fear or reverence.

As a counterword it has lost most of its meaning.

What word or words could you use instead of *awful* in the sentence, "It is awful stuffy in this room"?

2. In the previous sentence, the question mark went after the close quotes.

Sometimes the question mark goes before the close quotes. He said, "It is stuffy in here. Could anyone open a window?"

Given these two examples, give the rule as to where to put a question mark at the end of a quotation.

3. The next sentence in *Ducky* is:

At the computer store Ducky handed the salesman a coupon.

Name the case of each noun in that sentence.

·······**ANSWERS**·······

1. It is extremely stuffy in this room.

    It is quite stuffy in this room.

    It is unbearably stuffy in this room.

2. When the question mark (or the exclamation mark) is part of what was said, it goes inside of the quotation marks.

    She asked, "Is the pizza ready?"

    He shouted, "Stop!"

    When the question mark (or the exclamation mark) belongs to the whole sentence, it goes after the close quote.

    Was it she who said, "Let them eat cake"?

    In a quiet voice Ducky told the salesman, "I want to buy three computers"!

3. At the computer store Ducky handed the salesman a coupon.

          objective nominative   objective   objective

    In this sentence, *computer* is an adjective. In English, nouns are often used as adjectives: the *California* landscape, the *paper* towel, the *rubber* ducky.

Chapter Ten
Wolfie

Dubbo has a population of about 35,000. It's not a tiny town. Back in Kansas, there are lots of towns with fewer than a thousand inhabitants.* Tokyo, Japan, which, including its suburbs, has about 37,000,000 people, which is a thousand times larger than Dubbo.

---

* For example: Agra has a population of 265. Allen, 201. Alma, 745. Almena, 427. Alta Vista, 416. Altoona, 454. Americus, 877. Andale, 907. Arcadia, 385. Argonia, 468. Arlington, 434. Ashland, 855. Assaria, 446. Atlanta, 238. Attica, 570. Axtell, 415. Bazine, 333. Beattie, 258. Belvue, 224. Bennington, 612. Bentley, 526. Benton, 808. Bird City, 400. Bison, 202. Blue Mound, 275. Brewster, 251. Bronson, 338. Brookville, 263. Bucklin, 787. Buffalo, 266. Burden, 526. Burdett, 218. Burlingame, 942. Burns, 257. Burr Oak, 206. Burrton, 909. Bushton, 285. Canton, 786. Cawker City, 469. Cedar Vale, 612. Centralia, 479. Chase, 448. Cherokee, 717. Claflin, 633. Clifton, 492. Clyde, 669. Coldwater, 748. Colony, 372. Copeland, 325. Cottonwood Falls, 876. Countryside, 341. Courtland, 297. Cunningham, 444. Dearing, 394. Deerfield, 822. Delphos, 431. Denison, 224. Dexter, 336. Downs, 892. Dwight, 325. Eastborough, 811. Easton, 351. Edna, 412. Effingham, 569. Elbing, 208. Elk City, 295. Emmett, 269. Ensign, 201. Enterprise, 804. Eskridge, 562. Everest, 294. Fairview, 250. Florence, 591. Ford, 329. Fowler, 551. Frankfort, 771. Galva, 797. Garden Plain, 868. Gas, 527. Geneseo, 260. Glasco, 478. Glen Elder, 400. Goessel, 508. Gorham, 320. Grainfield, 268. Greeley, 317. Greenleaf, 310. Grenola, 212. Gridley, 349. Grinnell, 269. Gypsum, 404. Hamilton, 294. Hanover, 563. Hanston, 236. Hartford, 471. Harveyville, 250. Haviland, 424. Highland, 933. Holyrood, 444. Hope, 358. Howard, 746. Hoyt, 575. Ingalls, 329. Jamestown, 370. Jetmore, 826. Jewell, 396. Kanopolis, 504. Kanorado, 216. Kensington, 447. Kiowa, 892. Kirwin, 205. Kismet, 507. La Harpe, 250. Lake Quivira, 953. Lancaster, 287. Lane, 249. Le Roy, 550. Lebanon, 252. Lebo, 913. Lecompton, 666. Lenora, 267. Leon, 640. Leonardville, 437. Lewis, 444. Lincolnville, 201. Linn Valley, 568. Linn, 369. Linwood, 406. Little River, 521. Logan, 527. Longton, 362. Louisville, 210. Lucas, 407. Lyndon, 998. Macksville, 477. Madison, 729. Mankato, 773. Maple Hill, 501. Marquette, 581. Mayetta, 355. McCune, 423. McFarland, 272. McLouth, 823. Melvern, 405. Meriden, 748. Milford, 455. Miltonvale, 459. Minneola, 629. Moline, 419. Montezuma, 988. Moran, 521. Morrill, 244. Moscow, 237. Mound City, 762. Mound Valley, 406. Mount Hope, 872. Mulberry, 568. Natoma, 311. Neosho Rapids, 259. New Strawn, 396. Nortonville, 579. Norwich, 490. Olpe, 482. Onaga, 683. Otis, 293. Overbrook, 916. Ozawkie, 556. Palco, 210. Parker, 299. Partridge, 251. Pawnee Rock, 321. Paxico, 207. Perry, 836. Pomona, 942. Potwin, 434. Prescott, 265. Pretty Prairie, 602. Princeton, 330. Protection, 526. Quenemo, 425. Quinter, 761. Ransom, 268. Rantoul, 237. Reading, 231. Richmond, 497. Riley, 980. Rolla, 420. Scammon, 463. Scandia, 343. Schoenchen, 216. Scranton, 672. Severy, 319. Sharon Springs, 658. Smolan, 212. South Haven, 348. Spearville, 872. St. George, 589. St. Paul, 663. Strong City, 527. Sylvan Grove, 273. Sylvia, 292. Tescott, 324. Thayer, 482. Tipton, 228. Toronto, 262. Tribune, 660. Troy, 994. Turon, 428. Tyro, 219. Udall, 739. Uniontown, 277. Viola, 208. Wakefield, 898. Walnut, 219. Walton, 293. Waterville, 612. Waverly, 550. Weir, 706. West Mineral, 230. Westmoreland, 756. Westwood Hills, 369. Wetmore, 341. White City, 525. White Cloud, 222. Whitewater, 636. Whiting, 208. Williamsburg, 354. Wilson, 751. Winchester, 562. Woodbine, 206.
This footnote contains more than 140 examples of elliptical constructions.

"We're here," Margie said gently. Fred
opened his eyes. The
trip had taken ten
minutes.

Bob and Barbara's house

Margie parked in
front of the house.
When they got out of
the car, Fred noticed
the balcony. He had
never lived in a house with a balcony before.
Margie took Fred's hand and they walked to the
front door.

Before she could ring the bell, Barbara
opened the door and said, "Welcome." She
couldn't shake Fred's hand because he was
holding on to Margie's hand tightly. Barbara
said, "Come in and sit a while."

Barbara sat on a chair. Margie sat on the
couch, and Fred sat next to her. Fred was
feeling a little shy.

Barbara asked Fred,
"Do you like dogs? Do you
want to play with him?
His name is Wolfie."

Fred playing with Wolfie
(as Fred imagined it)

Wolfie! Fred thought.
I know what wolves are.
They are wild and strong.
A pack of them will attack

a sheep and eat it. I am much smaller than a sheep.

small essay

A Writer's Imagination

You will be a writer some day. You will write more than just grocery lists (pizza, chocolate milk, ribs, pizza, cheesecake, pizza). You will write to *convince*

to `inform` **or**

to **entertain.**

You will need what Fred has: an active imagination. All Barbara needed to do was mention her dog's name, and Fred pictured himself being consumed by a 600-pound wild animal.

As a writer, you will not *convince* anyone if you are dull.

You will not `inform` anyone if they fall asleep reading your words.

You will not **entertain** if you are boring.

❦ If you write a note to your sweetie, say more than just How R U?

❦ If you write a history textbook, don't just list a bunch of dates.

❦ If you write a book of prayers, say something that hasn't been heard a hundred times.[*]

Write words that sing, that laugh, that cry.

end of small essay

---

[*] In my *Prayers at 830* are the phrases, "You are all the love songs of the universe," "washing dishes in a hotel kitchen in Detroit," and "melted butter over potatoes."

Barbara called out, "Here Wolfie! Here Wolfie!"

Fred pulled his feet up onto the coach and sat on them. He didn't want them chewed off.

Wolfie

Suddenly, Fred's affect changed. He hopped off the couch and gave Wolfie a little pat on the head. Wolfie gave Fred a lick on his hand. They became instant friends.

Fred ran around the room and Wolfie ran around with him.

Margie stood up and said, "I guess it's time for me to go." She told Fred to enjoy himself at Barbara's. Fred hardly heard Margie's words; he was too busy playing with the dog.

After about ten minutes, the puppy got tired. He headed into another room to lie down. Fred went into the kitchen where Barbara was making lunch. She was preparing minestrone[*] soup.

---

[*] MIN-ə-STRO-knee   An Italian soup made with vegetables, beans, and pasta. Great with some Parmesan (PAR-mə-zan) cheese sprinkled on top. Perfect on a cold June day in Australia.

Minestrone came from the Latin word *ministrare*, which means to serve.

"Bob, <u>my husband</u>, will be back in a while. He's been out working in the barn."

Your Turn to Play

1. What is "my husband" called in language arts?
2. *Bob* is in which case?
3. *He has been working out in the barn* is in which tense?

4. Classify each of these examples below as an attempt to either *convince*, `inform`, or **entertain**.

Example A: An English teacher tells about the books Charles Dickens wrote. One of his most famous books is *David Copperfield.*

Example B: Joe tells Darlene that he can recite the alphabet backwards: zyxwvutsrqponmlkjihgfedcba.

Example C: Darlene wants Joe to marry her. She tells him that wedding cake tastes really good and you get a lot of presents on your wedding day.

. . . . ANSWERS . . . .

1. *My husband* is called an appositive (or an appositive phrase).

Here are some underlined appositive phrases:

    Fred Gauss, five-year-old
    Barbara, Bob's wife
    Barn worker Bob

2. *Bob* is the subject of the sentence. It is in the nominative case.

3. *Has been working* is in the present perfect progressive tense.

  ✓ The *ing* on *working* indicates progressive.

  ✓ The *been* indicates both perfect and progressive.

4. Example A: A teacher talking about the subject matter of the course is trying to `inform`.

When Fred teaches math at KITTENS University he also tries to be entertaining (by, for example, putting on costumes). He also tries to convince his students that math can be a lot of fun.

Example B: Joe is trying to **entertain** Darlene. He certainly isn't telling Darlene anything she didn't know before, and so he's not trying to inform.

Example C: When you are trying to change someone else's thoughts, you are trying to *convince*. Her talk about wedding cakes and presents might change Joe's attitude toward marrying her.

Chapter Eleven
Cooking

Fred braced himself for the usual questions that everyone seems to want to ask him when they first meet him. They want to know his name, his age, and where his parents are.

Barbara was different. "Do you know how to use a measuring cup? I need a half cup of  elbow macaroni." She handed him a measuring cup and a bag of macaroni.

She was busy making minestrone soup. With her sharp knife she sliced up a zucchini, a couple of carrots, a leek, a stalk of celery, and three tomatoes.

She handed him a can opener and a can of cannellini beans and a can of chicken broth. Fred was baffled. He had never used a can opener before. In fact, the whole process of cooking was foreign* to him. The only cooking

---

* *Foreign* does not obey the "I before E, except after C" rule. There is an exceptions sentence that some English teachers have their students memorize: The *weird* ones of *foreign leisure* could *neither seize* nor *forfeit* the *height*.

he had seen was when Stanthony made pizzas at his PieOne restaurant. (You'll read more about that restaurant in other *Life of Fred* books.)

Barbara showed Fred how to use the can opener.

She gave Fred a small block of Parmesan cheese and a grater.

While Fred was grating the cheese, she made a small pile of spices (thyme, basil, and oregano) and chopped them up. "It lets the flavor out," she told him.

She put everything except the Parmesan cheese into a large pot. She added some salt and a splash of olive oil and put the pot on the stove to heat. She asked him to put the Parmesan on the dining room table.

Fred thought *They sure do things different here in Australia. She's actually cooking food for lunch. In Kansas, food either comes out of the nine vending machines in the Math Building or it's a pizza from PieOne.**

"We've got about an hour before the soup is done," she said. "Let's go and get your room ready."

––––––––––––––––––––

* Fred was mistaken. There are actually some people in the United States who cook their food at home.

Fred didn't know what that meant. He was learning lots of things at Barbara's. The only way that he could think of making a room ready would be to put lots of interesting books on the shelves.

Fred followed her as she headed upstairs. He was hoping that his room would be the one with the balcony. It wasn't.

If I had written he hoped, *past tense, it would have had the same "flavor" as* Fred followed her.

If I had written he had hoped, *past perfect, it would have emphasized the fact that his hope had ended when he learned that there was no balcony.*

I wrote he was hoping, *past progressive, in order to stress the active nature of his hope.*

Of course, I could have written he had been hoping, *past perfect progressive, to indicate both that his hope had been dashed and that he was actively hoping.*

Time Out!

Fred had an active hope. *Hope* is a noun and *active* is an adjective that describes that noun.

What about words that describe the other parts of speech such as verbs or adjectives? Consider *actively hoping*. *Hoping* is a verb. *Actively* modifies *hoping*.

> *Actively* is an **adverb**. Adverbs and adjectives are brothers. Adjectives modify nouns (and pronouns). Adverbs modify everything else.
>
> If I write, "Curious Fred ran quickly," *curious* is an adjective because it describes the noun *Fred*. *Quickly* is an adverb because it modifies the verb *ran*.
>
> If I write, "He ran very quickly," *very* is an adverb. It modifies *quickly*, and *quickly* is not a noun.
>
> Adverbs are the seventh (and last!) of the seven parts of speech.

She entered a room at the end of the hall. Fred followed her. The room was bright (adjective) and smelled good (adverb).

Barbara stripped the sheets off the bed and handed them to Fred. She had guessed that Fred was about three years old and knew that he was old enough to start helping. It was more work *for her* to have Fred carry the sheets, but it was better *for Fred* to learn to take some responsibility. In other words, Barbara was a good mom whose goal was to point her kids toward adulthood. She wasn't their maid but their mentor.

Her mothering had three parts: (1) Lots of hugs, (2) Lots of play, and (3) Lots of opportunities to practice growing up. Every 14-year-old that Barbara mothered knew how to iron a shirt.

Your Turn to Play

The computer salesman quietly laughed.

1. Which are the adjectives and which are the adverbs in that sentence?

He gave Ducky the coupon and said, "This coupon is expired."

2. Label the case of each noun and pronoun. (nominative, possessive, objective)

3. What is the tense of each of the two verbs?

4. Change He gave Ducky the coupon into each of the eleven other tenses.

. . . . . . .ANSWERS . . . .

1. The   computer   salesman   quietly   laughed.
   adjective   adjective   adverb

The is an adjective. It modifies salesman. If you say *a salesman*, that had a different meaning than if you say *the salesman*.

2. He   gave Ducky the coupon and said, "This coupon is expired."
    nominative   objective   objective   nominative

3. *Gave* is in the past tense. *Is* is in the present tense.

4. Present   He gives Ducky the coupon.

    Present progressive   He is giving Ducky the coupon.

    Present perfect   He has given Ducky the coupon.

    Present perfect progressive   He has been giving Ducky the coupon.

    Past progressive   He was giving Ducky the coupon.

    Past perfect   He had given Ducky the coupon.

    Past perfect progressive   He had been giving Ducky the coupon.

    Future   He will give Ducky the coupon.

    Future progressive   He will be giving Ducky the coupon.

    Future perfect   He will have given Ducky the coupon.

    Future perfect progressive   He will have been giving Ducky the coupon.

Chapter Twelve
Cleaning

Fred carried the bed sheets down the stairs. He inadvertently (adverb) dropped the pillowcase. Barbara picked it up and quietly (adverb) handed it to him. Fred was heading straight (adverb) to the laundry room.

A Brief Note on the Way to the Laundry

I would bet that most people who have been speaking English all of their lives have never noticed that adverbs ending in –ly often come before the verbs they modify, and the other adverbs come after the verbs they modify.

We don't say, "handed quietly it to him," or "was straight heading to the laundry room."

Barbara opened the washing machine door, and Fred stuffed the sheets inside.

There were three measuring cups in the laundry powder, a half cup, a third cup, and a quarter cup.

Barbara said, "Margie, the social worker, (appositive) told me that you claimed to be a university math teacher." Barbara tried not to giggle when she said that.

"Did you have a math question?" Fred

asked. He didn't understand that Barbara
didn't believe he was a teacher.

"Okay," she said. "Here's a really tough
problem. Using these measuring cups, could
you put one cup of laundry powder into the
machine?"

That's tough? Fred thought incredulously.*
She's gotta be kidding. He said, "You could use
two half cups or three third cups or four quarter
cups."

Then Fred asked her, "Let's get a little
tougher. Using those measuring cups, could you
put five-sixths of a cup into the machine?"

Barbara got out a piece of paper and tried
various combinations.

$$\frac{1}{2} + \frac{1}{4} = \frac{2}{4} + \frac{1}{4} = \frac{3}{4} \quad \text{That doesn't work.}$$

$$\frac{1}{3} + \frac{1}{4} = \frac{4}{12} + \frac{3}{12} = \frac{7}{12} \quad \text{That doesn't work.}$$

$$\frac{1}{2} + \frac{1}{3} = \frac{3}{6} + \frac{2}{6} = \frac{5}{6} \quad \text{Yes!}$$

"That's not so hard," she said. "Just put in
a half of a cup and a third of a cup."

---

* Incredulous (in-KREJ-ə-ləs) means not believing. Adverbs ending
in *—ly* do not *have* to go in front of the verbs they modify.

    Quickly he solved the problem.

    He *quickly* solved the problem.

    He solved the problem *quickly*.

Fred smiled and said, "That was just a warm-up question. With those measuring cups can you measure one-twelfth ($\frac{1}{12}$) of a cup? I can."

"Ha!" she said as she handed him a dustcloth. She carried the vacuum cleaner and they headed back to his bedroom. She knew that this little kid was just talking nonsense. Margie had warned her that he liked to tell tall tales. Fred wasn't given the chance to show Barbara how to do it.

Barbara turned on the vacuum, and Fred stood there holding the dustcloth. He had never used one before and wasn't sure what to do.

He *plopped* it on his head to make a hat.

He *slapped* the pillow with the cloth.

He was *working* as hard as he could.

It *occurred* to him that he was unsure.

He *despaired*.

He *opened* the dustcloth to look for instructions.

Smacking the cloth on the wall made a funny sound.

The thought of playing outside *beckoned* to him.

He *folded* the cloth.

Wait a minute! I, your reader, can't figure out what you are trying to do. Why are you writing all

these simple sentences and *italicizing* **the verbs? What's the point?**

Do you remember what a consonant is?

Sure. Everybody knows it is a non-vowel.

All of the *italicized* words end in a consonant.

Big deal.

I'm not done.

Some of these double their final consonant when you add an ending:

> plop → plopped
>
> slap → slapped
>
> occur → occurred

And some do *not* double their final consonant when you add an ending:

> work → working
>
> despair → despaired
>
> open → opened
>
> smack → smacking
>
> beckon → beckoned
>
> fold → folded

I suspect that there is some rule governing when to double the final consonant.

> suspect → suspected
>
> govern → governing

Yes there is, but there isn't room on this page to tell you.

Okay. There's plenty of room on this page!

Many English books make a big mess when they try to explain the doubling-consonant rule. Please do not read this if you want to stay sane:

#1. If it is a one-syllable word and if there is exactly one vowel that proceeds the consonant, then double the final consonant. For example, tip → tipped.

#2. If it is a one-syllable word and if there are two vowels that proceed the consonant, then do not double the final consonant. For example, read → reading.

#3. If it is a one-syllable word and if there is a consonant that proceeds the final consonant, then do not double the final consonant. For example, quack → quacked.

#4. If it has more than one syllable and there is exactly one vowel that proceeds the consonant and if the word is accented on the last syllable, then double the final consonant. For example, submit → submitted.

#5. If it has more than one syllable and if there are two vowels that proceed the final consonant, then do not double the final consonant. For example, despair → despairing.

#6. If it has more than one syllable and if there is a consonant that proceeds the final consonant, then do not double the final consonant. For example, debunk → debunked.

#7. If there is more than one syllable and the accent does not fall on the last syllable after the ending has been added, then do not double the final consonant. For example, beckon → beckoning.

No English book that I've encountered could boil it down to a single rule: *Double the final consonant when two things are true: there is a single vowel before the single final consonant and the accent falls on the last syllable after you have added the ending.*

Your Turn to Play

1. Add an *-ing* to each of these verbs.

dust

refer

transmit

kneel

swim

debit

```
. . . . . . . ANSWERS . . . . . . .
```

1.

   dusting

   referring

   transmitting

   kneeling

   swimming

   debiting

Don't double the *y* in verbs ending in *y*.

portray → portraying

play → playing

———————•••••——————

Barbara didn't believe that it was possible to use her measuring cups to measure one-twelfth of a cup. Here's how to do it.

Fill the one-third cup.

Pour as much of that into the one-quarter cup as possible.

What's left in the one-third cup is one-twelfth of a cup.

$$\frac{1}{3} - \frac{1}{4} = \frac{4}{12} - \frac{3}{12} = \frac{1}{12}$$

Chapter Thirteen
How to Dust

Barbara took the dustcloth out of Fred's hand and showed him how to use it. She explained that you first rub it on some dusty surface and then you open the window and shake it out. She handed the cloth back to him and continued her vacuuming.

Fred tried to rub the cloth on the mattress. She stopped vacuuming and told him that you only dust hard surfaces.

He took one swipe at a tabletop and started to head toward the window. She shouted over the noise of the vacuum, "Dust for about a minute before you head to the window."

Fred thought *This was all much more complicated than doing math. When I was teaching about the intersection of two sets, I would first list two sets such as {✂, ★, 5} and {★, 7, ☎}, and then just say that the intersection was the set that contains things that were in both sets. {✂, ★, 5} ∩ {★, 7, ☎} = {★}. Using a dust*

the intersection symbol

cloth is a lot more complicated. You have to remember about hard surfaces, about not shaking the cloth after every swipe, about making sure the window is open.

Fred counted to 60 as he dusted the tabletop, the chairs, and the doorknob. After about a minute had passed, he went to the window. He made sure the window was open and began to shake out the cloth.

He wasn't holding the cloth tightly enough. It was gone.

Barbara stopped vacuuming. She thought he had thrown the cloth out the window. Fred shrugged his little shoulders and said, "It slipped."

He headed down the stairs and through the kitchen. The minestrone soup in the kitchen smelled good. He headed outside and found the dustcloth lying in the dirt.* He picked it up. It was dirty.

He thought about all the instructions Barbara had given him:

1. Find a dusty surface.
2. Dust only hard surfaces.
3. Dust for about a minute.
4. Open the window.
5. Shake the dustcloth.   (She had forgotten to include, 6. Hold on tight.)

If Fred had been a little more experienced in cleaning, she would have probably given him *less* instructions . . . or is it *fewer* instructions?

---

* *Laying* is a transitive verb. It needs an object. If Fred had dropped a chicken out the window, he might have found the chicken *laying* eggs in the dirt.

Lots of people mix up *less* and *fewer*. The rule is simple: If you can count them one by one, use *fewer*.

Barbara might have given *fewer* instructions if Fred were more experienced in cleaning.

Fred would have been *less* confused if he had done dusting before.

Less heat would make the soup cook more slowly.

Fewer tomatoes in the soup would make it *less* tasty.

Less salt might mean *less* blood pressure and *fewer* strokes.*

He wondered what to do with a dustcloth that had been (past perfect) dropped in the dirt. Most

---

* Question: Do rules in English have exceptions?
  Question: Does the sun come up at dawn?
  Question: Does *less* have fewer letters than *fewer*?
     Yes, yes, and yes.
     The exceptions to the less/fewer rule often occur in dealing with time or money. It is correct to say, "She ran the race in less than six hours." It might have taken her five hours and 32 minutes.
     If we learned, "She ran the race in fewer than six hours," that would indicate that we are counting the hours, one-by-one. To say "fewer than six hours" would mean either five or four or three hours.
     $9.96 is less than ten dollars.

people would have shaken the cloth before bringing it back into the house. Fred was trying (past progressive) to please Barbara and follow her instructions. He was going to take it into the house, up the stairs, and shake it out the window.

He had locked himself out.

Back at his math office in Kansas, he would have simply unlocked the door with his key. Here, he didn't have a key.

If he knocked on the door, Barbara probably wouldn't hear it because she was upstairs vacuuming.

If he rang the doorbell, then she would have to stop vacuuming, come downstairs, and let him in. He wondered if that would make her angry. He had already been shy, been frightened of Wolfie, and been unable to use a can opener. He had dropped the pillowcase he was carrying, gave her a math question she couldn't solve ($\frac{1}{3} - \frac{1}{4} = \frac{1}{12}$), made her stop vacuuming to tell him to dust only hard surfaces, made her shout that he should dust for a minute before shaking out the cloth, and had thrown the dustcloth out the window.

Fred didn't realize that Barbara had been a foster parent to many little kids over the years. It's normal for them to make mistakes. It's just part of being human. Barbara was good at forgiveness.

    Fred thought *I have the perfect solution. She had said that Bob, her husband, would soon be back from the barn. I'll just wait for him. He can let me in.*

    While we're waiting . . .

Your Turn to Play

1. Copy each of these phrases and insert either *less* or *fewer*. (As usual, please do not write in this book.)

       ___?___ choices

       ___?___ dustcloths

       ___?___ noise

       ___?___ days

       ___?___ time

2. $\{4, ♪, ✖, ☆\} \cap \{✖, 9, ☆, W, ✡\} = \ ?$

3. Disappointed Ducky unhappily received the expired coupon.

    Which are the adjectives and which are the adverbs?

4. After he had pocketed the expired coupon, he still wanted a computer.

    What are the tenses of the two verbs?

    What part of speech is *still* in that sentence?

......ANSWERS......

1.   fewer choices   You can count the choices.

   fewer dustcloths   There can be three or four dustcloths.

   less noise   You can't have three noises.

   fewer days

   less time

2. $\{4, ♪, ✖, ☆\} \cap \{✖, 9, ☆, W, ☼\} = \{✖, ☆\}$

This is true because ✖ and ☆ are the two things that are in both sets.

3. Disappointed Ducky unhappily received the expired coupon.
   adjective   adverb   adjective

4. After he had pocketed the expired coupon, he still
                    past perfect

wanted a computer.
   past tense

The perfect tenses indicate an action that has stopped. Ducky had completed the action of stuffing the coupon in his pocket, and then he did something else (wanted the computer).

Still modifies the verb *wanted*. It is acting as an adverb.

Still can act as an adjective, e.g., the still waters.

Still can act as a noun. A still is an apparatus used for distilling.

Still can act as a conjunction. It was hopeless, still he tried.

Still can act as a verb. He stilled the waters.

He should be wearing eye protection!

Chapter Fourteen
Infinitives

Fred waited. And waited. And waited. Bob didn't come. Fred stood there with his dirty dustcloth in his hand. He heard voices coming from inside the house.

(Barbara's voice) I wonder where our new kid is. He threw the dustcloth out the window and went to fetch it.

(Some man's voice) I haven't seen him.

(Barbara's voice) He's about three years old and doesn't seem to know much. I had to teach him how to use a dust rag.

(Some man's voice) I've been here in the house for the last ten minutes. I was washing up downstairs. I thought I heard you and the kid upstairs when you shouted, "Dust for a minute before heading to the window."

Fred figured out what had happened. Bob wouldn't be coming because he had already come.

 Suddenly Wolfie was standing right next to Fred. That surprised him. He thought Wolfie was inside the house.

"How did you get outside?" he asked the puppy.

Fred noticed the doggie door, which was a little door that had been cut into the front door. It was so small that Wolfie could fit through it, but no burglar could ever squeeze through it.

Wolfie ran back into the house through the doggie door. Fred easily followed him.

Fred ran up the stairs to his bedroom. He shook the dustcloth out of the window. This time he held onto the cloth tightly. He folded the cloth neatly and put it <u>on the table</u>.

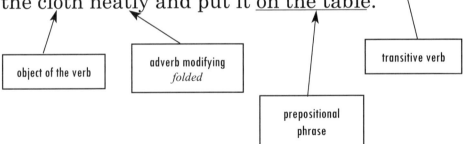

object of the verb

adverb modifying *folded*

transitive verb

prepositional phrase

Fred ran downstairs to meet Bob.

Some notes about that sentence.

♪#1: *To meet* is the **infinitive** form of the verb *meet*. Infinitive forms of verbs are easy to recognize: to sing, to laugh, to run, to think, etc.

♪#2: The infinitive form of a verb is not attached to any time, person, or number. It is the purest form of the verb. The best example is *to be*. Once you attach *to be* to a time (he is, he was) or attach it to a person (I am, you are, she is), or attach it to a number (I am, we are), it changes a lot.*

♪#3: We have talked about changing nouns into adjectives (*Texas* oil wells, *paper* towels). We have talked about changing verbs into adjectives by adding suffixes (sing → singable, fear → fearless).

♪#4: The infinitive form of a verb will change a verb into lots of other parts of speech. It depends on how it is used in a sentence.

>   Infinitive form used as a subject of a sentence:
>>   *To teach* is Fred's delight in life.

>   Infinitive form used as an object of a transitive verb:
>>   Joe likes *to fish*.

>   Infinitive form used as an adjective:
>>   Darlene had wedding plans *to make*.

>   Infinitive form used as an adverb:
>>   Fred ran downstairs *to meet* Bob.

The phrase "to meet Bob" describes the purpose for Fred's running. It modifies *ran*.

Bob shook Fred's hand. That felt very much like how some adults greet each other. Fred had never shaken hands with any of his students or with the police officer or with Margie, the social worker. That make Fred feel more like an adult. He felt taller.

---

* *Alot* is not a word!

Barbara asked him, "Do you know how to set a table?" She handed him some knives, forks, and spoons.

Fred tried to think of how the silverware was laid out at Stanthony's PieOne restaurant. That's the only place where he had seen knives, forks, and spoons. At Stanthony's they came wrapped up in a paper napkin with a paper tape holding them together.

Barbara had already put the holloware* on the table. Fred put a knife, fork, and spoon in each bowl.

Bob tried not to laugh, but failed.** He said, "Didn't your mother ever teach you how to set a table?"

Fred shook his head. He couldn't even think of a time when he and his parents all sat down at a table and ate a meal together.

"You put the fork on the left of the bowl," he began.

Fred almost got it right. Bob turned the fork around.

---

* Holloware = bowls and glasses—those items that have volume. Flatware = knives, forks, spoons, plates, and saucers.

** Translation: He laughed.

Bob said, "And you put the knife and spoon on the right of the bowl."

Fred almost got it right.

"And the knife goes next to the bowl, and the edge of the knife faces left."

Fred got it right.

Your Turn to Play

In each of these sentences, is the infinitive form used as A) the subject of the sentence

   B) the object of a transitive verb

   C) an adjective or

   D) an adverb

1. Fred learned to set the table.
2. To point the fork in the right direction is important.
3. Fred set the table to please his foster parents.
4. Fred attempted to do it right.
5. He had plenty of forks to work with.

. . . . ANSWERS . . . .

1. B) the object of a transitive verb

    Fred learned to set the table.

    He learned *what?*

    To set the table is the object of the verb *learned.*

2. A) the subject of the sentence

    To point the fork in the right direction is important.

    Something is important.

    Something is the subject of the sentence.

3. D) an adverb

    Fred set the table to please his foster parents.

    Why did he set the table? *What* was his *purpose?*

4. B) the object of a transitive verb

    Fred attempted to do it right.

    Attempted is a transitive verb.

    He was attempting *something.*

5. C) an adjective

    He had plenty of forks to work with.

    How would you describe that phrase *plenty of forks?*

    They weren't just forks in the drawer. They were
    the forks that Fred had control over.

   Every book on English has to deal with prepositions at
the end of sentences. I could have written, ". . . the forks over
which Fred had control," but that would sound awkward. In
normal idiomatic English, you don't say, "To whom are you
speaking?"

Chapter Fifteen
Know What You're Saying

Bob and Fred sat down. Fred stared at the empty bowl in front of him. It looked immense, huge, capacious,* and large.**

He thought *I hope she doesn't ask me how hungry I am. I might be able to eat only one bean in the minestrone soup. Or maybe a half of a bean. That must be what the knife and fork are for.*

The bowl wasn't really that large.

Barbara didn't ask Fred how hungry he was. She just filled his bowl. She did say, "And don't worry. We've got plenty if you want seconds."

Bob held up his teaspoon and smiled.

Barbara exclaimed, "Goodness gracious! You can't eat soup with a teaspoon." She removed the teaspoons from the table and replaced them with soup spoons.

That made it even worse for Fred.

---

* cap-PAY-shəs capacious = capable of holding a lot

** My thesaurus in action.

Goodness gracious is an exclamation of surprise. It is also a **minced oath**.

small essay

The Meaning of Your Words

A **euphemism** (YOU-fə-MIZ-əm) is the substitution of a mild expression for one that is offensive or blunt. Instead of saying *he died*, you euphemistically might say *he passed away* or *he cashed in his chips* or *he went to meet his Maker*.

In the English language most impolite words have euphemisms. The euphemisms for swear words are called minced oaths.

You take the original words and mispronounce or misspell them in order to be less offensive.

Instead of *hell*, the minced oath might be *heck* or *H-E-double toothpicks*.

Many older Southern women say *Goodness gracious* and don't realize that it is a euphemism for the grace of God.

In the Looney Tunes and Merrie Melodies cartoons, you never hear profanity, but Sylvester the cat loves to say *suffering succotash*. That's a minced oath for *suffering Savior*.

end of small essay

Fred used his soup spoon to look for a bean in his soup. He found a piece of carrot. He put it on his spoon. *That's more than a mouthful* he thought. He set the spoon down and picked up his knife and fork in order to cut that tiny piece of carrot into many smaller pieces.

"Good grief! (minced oath) What are you doing?" Bob exclaimed. "Stop playing with your food."

Fred hadn't been playing. It was real work to attempt to use a knife and fork to cut a piece of carrot that is sitting in a spoon. The spoon kept jumping around as he tried to slice through the carrot.

"If I were you," said Barbara, "I'd get back to eating. We've got lots of things to do this afternoon."

small essay
Not "If I *Was* You"

Welcome to the wonderful world of the **subjunctive mood**! This is not another tense. We have already done the 12 tenses.

There are three moods in English. Two of them you know already.

The **indicative mood** is used 98% of the time. You use it whenever you state a fact, an opinion, or ask a question.

> Rectangles have four sides. [fact]
> Math is easier than English. [opinion]
> Why does Fred eat so little? [question]

The **imperative mood** is used to give directions or commands.

> Stop playing with your food. [command]
> Use the third door on the left. [direction]

It's easy to tell if something is in the imperative mood. The subject of the sentence is missing.

The **subjunctive mood** can be used to indicate something that is:

∗ not true

   ∗ desired

      ∗ a suggestion

         ∗ doubtful or

            ∗ required

I wish I *were* a rich man.

It is our desire that Heaven *help* us.

It is required that the report *be* submitted today.

She should *sing* tomorrow.

The subjunctive mood is alive and well in German and French (the two languages I studied in school). In my German textbook (I still have it) two of the 15 chapters were devoted to learning the two forms of the subjunctive mood! For the subjunctive II form, the book explained: The subjunctive II is built on past indicative forms. If the verb whose subjunctive form is to be used is strong or is a modal auxiliary, its stem vowel, a, o, or u is usually modified to ä, ö or ü. The ending -e is added in the *ich, er, sie, es* forms; -en in the *wir, sie, Sie* forms.

In English the subjunctive mood seems to be dying a slow death. In all the *Life of Fred* language arts books, this little essay may be the only mention of the subjunctive mood.

In correct, formal English: "If you *be* quiet, you might hear the train coming" or "If it *be* cold, we will go to the movies."

(The subjunctive uses a lot of be's and were's.)

In general English, we often switch to the indicative mood and say, "If you are quiet, you might hear the train coming."

The other way of avoiding the subjunctive is to switch to other forms of the verb. Instead of "She required that he *stay* home," you might have, "She required him to stay home."

Instead of "She insisted that he *go* with her," you might have, "She insisted on his going with her."

end of small essay

Your Turn to Play

1. (True ⇨) Many people (myself included) who start a small business find that excessive government is their biggest obstacle to success. Last week I heard, "Heavy taxes be hanged!"

What *two* things from this chapter are at work here?

2. (True ⇨) I have one half-time employee. The government requires that I submit 15 tax forms (three each quarter and three at the end of the year) because I employ him.

In the following sentence, is the infinite form used as the subject, the object, an adjective, or an adverb?

I have 15 forms to fill out.

3. (Continuing the *Ducky Sings Opera* story . . .)

Ducky handed the clerk a very large wad of cash and left with a new computer.

Are there any adverbs in that sentence?

Are any of the nouns in the objective case? (See Chapter 7)

· · · · · · ·ANSWERS· · · · · · ·

1. "Heavy taxes be hanged!"

❶ *To be hanged* is a minced oath. Since I do not use profanity in this book, all I can say is that *to be hanged* means to be sent to heck by golly.

❷ *Heavy taxes be hanged!* indicates a desire and something that is currently not true. It is in the subjunctive mood.

If it were in the indicative mood,

in the present tense   Heavy taxes are hanged.

in the past tense   Heavy taxes were hanged.

in the future tense   Heavy taxes will be hanged.

These three are called the simple tenses.

Using the right word . . .
People are hanged.
Pictures are hung.

2. *To fill out* modifies *forms*. It describes those particular forms. If I go to the government tax offices, I can find hundreds of forms, but these 15 forms are the ones that I have *to fill out*.

To fill out is a phrase that acts as an adjective modifying the noun *forms*.

3. I see one adverb: *very*. It modifies the adjective *large*.

Ducky handed the clerk a very large wad of cash and left with a new computer.

From Chapter 7: Direct and indirect objects and the objects of prepositions are in the objective case.

clerk is an indirect object.

wad is a direct object

cash and computer are in prepositional phrases.

Chapter Sixteen
What Wolfie Ate

The spoon slipped onto Fred's lap. The tiny piece of carrot hit the floor. Wolfie ate it.

Meaning

English has a lot of ambiguity. (AM-bi-gyoo-ity = there are several possible meanings)

We hardly give a second thought to how sloppy language is.

I wrote *Wolfie ate it.* *It* is a pronoun. To what does it refer? The closest noun is *floor*, but you didn't think that Wolfie ate the floor. Instead you assumed he ate the carrot.

Carrot is the **antecedent** of *it*. ANN-tə-SEED-nt   *ante* is a prefix which means *comes before*. Antebellum means before the war. Antedate means an older date. Antemeridian means before noon. But antelope does not

mean before the lope. It means

Some day I'll write an essay about the proper use of antecedents.

small essay

The Proper Use of Pronouns and Their Antecedents

Pronouns should point back to a clear antecedent. If your friend walks up to you and says, "I have just learned that he will join us at the movies this afternoon," the question that pops into your mind is, "Whom is my friend referring to?"

Each pronoun needs to point to a definite antecedent. Consider: "Jane told Joan that *she* was smart." It is not clear who the pronoun *she* refers to.

Consider: "The word *vexillology* has five syllables. It deals with the study of flags." What does the *it* in the second sentence refer to? Revise the second sentence: "Vexillology deals with the study of flags."

Consider: "Fred petted Wolfie's head who was standing by Fred's chair." *Who* is a pronoun, but its antecedent is not clear. Revised: "Fred petted the head of Wolfie who was standing by Fred's chair."

Consider: "Chris was attacked by a shark, but *it* was not serious."

end of small essay

Ha! Ha! Ha!
a non-serious shark

Fred put the spoon back into the soup. He despaired. Fred felt so alone in the world. Everyone else he knew ate morning, noon, and night. To him it seemed like such a waste of time—time that could be spent doing math, or jogging, or singing. It didn't seem to make much sense spending hours chewing and swallowing.

"My tummy hurts," Fred told his foster parents. "No more soup."

Barbara and Bob were experienced foster parents. They had taken care of many kids over the years. Four possibilities popped into their minds.

① The most likely case is that he had spoiled his appetite by eating candy or drinking soda before they sat down to eat. Some three-year-olds will lie and say their tummy hurts as an excuse not to eat. They didn't know that Fred doesn't lie.

Barbara asked Fred, "What have you eaten in the last couple hours?"

Fred shook his head and said, "Nothing."

② The second most likely reason why a child will say that he's not hungry is that he wants to save room for lots of dessert.

Barbara asked Fred, "Are you waiting for the boysenberry pie that I baked?"

Fred shook his head. "No pie. Thank you."

③ Sometimes kids get tummy aches when they've eaten some spoiled food.

Bob asked Fred, "Are you nauseous?"

Barbara simplified the question, "Do you think you might throw up?"

Fred answered Barbara's question first. "No, I'm not nauseated."

Then he turned to Bob and said, "You can never really ask someone else if they're nauseous. That's something that only you can decide."

Bob didn't understand. "I don't get it.*"

Fred explained, "To be nauseated means to be ready to vomit. Barbara had to ask me if I were (subjunctive mood) feeling like I was ready to throw up.

"*Nauseous* means something that is sickening, something that makes *you* want to toss your cookies (= throw up, upchuck, puke, barf)."

Barbara understood. She explained to Bob, "Do you remember Uncle Ralph's cigars? They were nauseous to me, and you said that you liked the smell."

 MORAL: *You should never ask someone if they are nauseous.* *That's up to you to decide.* Nurses especially, please pay attention!

---

* This is spoken English, not formal English. In formal English, Bob might have said, "I do not understand what you are saying."

  The antecedent of *it* in "I don't get it," is the words that Fred has just spoken.

  When a pronoun refers to an idea rather than to a specific noun, we say that it has a **broad reference**.

④   The least likely possibility was that Fred had appendicitis. The suffix *itis* means an inflamation or disease.

Biology time!

     If your appendix gets swollen and full of pus, you have appendicitis. Your appendix looks like a 3½-inch worm. It is a pouch located where the small intestine meets the large intestine. It's on the right side of your body, a couple of inches down and to the right of your navel (bellybutton).

     What good does an appendix do? Not much, as far as we can tell. What bad does it do? One person out of about every 500 gets an attack of appendicitis each year and that is a medical emergency. Medical emergency = you get to the doctor . . . now.

     The symptoms are a severe pain. Even a slight touch over the spot makes the pain even worse. Also may feel feverish and nauseated (not nauseous!) Doctors can tell whether its an appendicitis or not, and they know how to fix it.

Your Turn to Play

1. Appendicitis is an inflamation of the appendix.

     Correct this pronoun-antecedent error: She had an attack of appendicitis. It burst before she got to the doctor.

2. Revise: Doctors can fix an attack of appendicitis easily if she can get to it before the appendix bursts.

3. (Continuing the *Ducky Sings Opera* story . . .)
     The clerk took Ducky's money and put it into the cash register.

     Which case is each noun and pronoun in that sentence—nominative, possessive, or objective?

1. She had an attack of appendicitis. It broke before she got to the doctor. The *it* can't refer to appendicitis. Diseases don't burst.

   One possible revision: She had an attack of appendicitis. Her appendix burst before she got to the doctor.

2. The *it* in the sentence—Doctors can fix an attack of appendicitis easily if she can get to it before the appendix bursts.—is okay. That *it* refers to *attack*.

   The problem is the pronoun *she*. *She* is singular, but it is referring to *doctors*, which is plural.

   One possible revision: Doctors can fix an attack of appendicitis easily if they can get to it before the appendix bursts.

   Second possible revision: My doctor can fix an attack of appendicitis easily if she can get to it before the appendix bursts.

3. The clerk took Ducky's money and put it into the cash register.
   nominative   possessive   objective   objective   objective

   Cash in this sentence is an adjective that modifies *register*.

Cash can also be a noun: We accept cash.

Cash can also be a verb: Please cash this check.

Chapter Seventeen
A Fifth Alternative

All four of Barbara and Bob's guesses were wrong. Fred hadn't spoiled his appetite with candy. He wasn't waiting for dessert. He hadn't eaten spoiled food. And he didn't have appendicitis.

There was a fifth alternative: hunger pangs. Fred's tummy was saying, "Feed me!" He had never made the connection between the pain that he had in his stomach* and the fact that he seldom ate.

Everyone is smart in some areas and dumb in others. Fred was good in math. He knew that 2^{10} equals 1024, but he couldn't tell a hunger pang from a hangnail. (2^{10} means $2 \times 2 \times 2 \times 2 \times 2 \times 2 \times 2 \times 2 \times 2 \times 2$) For almost everyone, it will always

---

*Have you ever wondered why *stomach* isn't spelled stumik? That would make a lot more sense.

What can we do about that? Nothing really. It is a fact of life that *stomach* is spelled s-t-o-m-a-c-h. If you start spelling it stumik, people might think that you are stewped.

It is a fact of life that the keys on a keyboard are arranged as they are. (People over the years have suggested more logical arrangements of keys, but QWERTYUIOP remains.)

It is a fact of life that if you decide to become a medical doctor, all of your patients will eventually die. (It's much better to become a teacher. Some of your students eventually learn!)

seem true that what other people can do is much more amazing than what you can do. A hundred lifetimes would be much too short to learn to do everything well:

★ speak Japanese

★ be a ballet star

★ learn to spell *stomach*

★ parent kids with love

★ know everything about roses

★ write great poems

This list is not complete.

Life consists of two parts.
First, finding what you
    are good at,
    like to do, and
    is worthwhile.
Second, doing it.

Both parts are **hard**. Finding what you are good at/like to do/is worthwhile usually takes decades. Doing it takes dedication. It means not wasting a lot of time watching television, etc.

Bob finished his soup and then finished Fred's soup. Fred brought the empty bowls into the kitchen. He wanted to be a good son.

Barbara cut pieces of boysenberry pie for herself and her husband.

Fred came back to the table. He was glad they weren't forcing him to eat. He was thinking:*

Boysenberry pie . . . I'm sure glad that Rudolph Boysen created that berry back in the 1920s. He crossed a European raspberry, a blackberry, and a Loganberry . . . Boysenberry pie wouldn't be the same without Boysen's berries. Pie. That's not the same as pi (π). I taught a lot about pi in my math classes

---

* What comes next is Fred's interior monologue, his inner thoughts. This is called **stream of consciousness** writing. It's like living in someone else's brain.

Robinson Crusoe was the first novel that I ever read. I lived with the hero in his adventures on a desert island as I read what he was thinking.

In contrast, I hated (personal opinion) the stream of consciousness in James Joyce's *Ulysses*. This is from page 642:

a quarter after what an unearthly hour I suppose they're just getting up in China now combing out their pigtails for the day well soon have the nuns ringing the angelus they've nobody coming in to spoil their sleep except an odd priest or two for his night office or the alarmlock next door at cockshout clattering the brain out of itself let me see if I can doze off 1 2 3 4 5 what kind of flowers are those they invented like the stars the wallpaper in Lombard street was much nicer the apron he gave me was like that something only I only wore it twice better lower this lamp and try again so that I can get up early back at KITTENS University. In calculus* I prove that the area of an ellipse is equal to abπ. I'm sure glad I teach math and not English. WAIT! (panic) I do teach English.

I have classes at Dubbo School of English. Right now!

Fred stood up. He had to get back to Dubbo. "Please excuse me," he said to Barbara and Bob.

He headed out the front door (and locked himself out again). He looked around and realized that he had no idea where he was. He had been napping when Margie had driven him to Bob and Barbara.

Where's Dubbo?

---

* *Life of Fred: Calculus*, pp. 135–136

He turned back and found that the door was locked. As Fred crawled through the doggie door Wolfie licked his nose. Wolfie had the smell of boysenberry pie on his breath.

Your Turn to Play

1. Proofread this next part of the *Ducky Sings Opera* story. Each paragraph has two errors.

Ducky easily carried his computer It didn't way that much.

He sat his computer down on the side walk.

He knew something was wrong. Opening the back of the computer, a half-eaten sanwich fell out.

2. Revise (to correct the pronoun-antecedent error):
In *Robinson Crusoe,* you read about when he meets another man on the island.

3. What are the moods of these three underlined verbs?

Name the six most common ways to cook hamburgers. If I were you, I would write my answers very neatly.

· · · · · · · ANSWERS · · · · · · ·

1.   Ducky easily carried his computer It didn't way that much.

insert a period
Sentences end with a period, question mark, or exclamation mark.

weigh
spelling error

He sat his computer down on the side walk.

set
The verb *sat* is not a transitive verb.

sidewalk
spelling error

He knew something was wrong. Opening the back of the computer, a half-eaten sanwich fell out.

When he opened the back of the computer
The sandwich didn't open the back of the computer.

sandwich
The word has a silent *d*.

2. *Robinson Crusoe* is the name of the book. The book couldn't meet another man on the island.

One possible revision: In *Robinson Crusoe*, you read about when Robinson meets another man on the island.

3. Name the six most common ways to cook hamburgers. If I were you, I would write my answers very neatly.

Name is in the imperative mood. *Were* is in the subjunctive mood. The tricky one is the verb *write*. This verb indicates a desire or suggestion. It is also in the subjunctive mood.

Chapter Eighteen
Missing Hyphens

All that Fred could say to Barbara and Bob was, "I need to get to the Dubbo School of English." They thought that he wanted to become a student at the school.

Barbara said, "That school is for older kids. You are only three years old. The only exception they make is for two-year-old Suzie and her kangaroo, Hoppy. Suzie is the only one in the ten o'clock class."

Fred remembered how bright Suzie was.

"In any event," Barbara continued, "I just heard on the radio. They have shut the school down."

What? Fred thought to himself. Why? He asked, "Did it burn down?"

"No. The radio said that the school storage shed burned down, but the school itself was not harmed. The mystery was what happened to the teacher for the school. He was a volunteer from America, and he just disappeared."

Bob said, "Maybe the noon news will fill in the details." He turned on the television.

It was an old television that took a minute to warm up.

The first thing they saw was a commercial. That is not unusual.*

"Wow! How can they do that?" Bob exclaimed. "Trees that are a hundred years old would have to cost a fortune."

"That's incredible," Barbara said. "We have to get there before all those old trees are sold."

Fred said, "But, but, but …" but his words were ignored.

Bob picked up Fred. He was surprised how light he was, and all four of them headed to the family car.

Bob put Fred in the backseat and Wolfie joined him. They headed off to the big tree sale.

---

* This is an example of litotes—using *not* with the opposite of what you intend to say. Instead of saying, "Finding a commercial on television is not unusual," you could say, "Commercials on television are very, very common."

   Or, using a simile (Chapter 7), you could say, "Finding a commercial on television is like finding water in the ocean."

Barbara said, "I wonder how tall those trees are. Maybe we should have brought our truck. I remember the commercial saying that they were big trees."

Fred said, "Hyphen, hyphen, hyphen," but no one listened to him.

"You're right," Bob said. "If those trees are a hundred years old, we wouldn't even be able to get one of them in our car."

Fred finally spoke up a little louder. "I bet they are all about 15 centimeters* tall."

Bob laughed at him.

"Boy, didn't they ever teach you about the metric system. You meant 15 meters, not centimeters. A meter** is a little longer than a yard."

Barbara said, "We probably couldn't even get one of those big trees in our truck. They probably offer shipping."

---

* 15 cm ≈ 6 inches. Fred used metric because he wasn't in America. The easiest conversion factor to memorize is two inches almost exactly equals five centimeters.

** 1 meter ≈ 39 inches.

They arrived at the big sale.

Fred was wrong. They weren't six inches (15 cm) tall; they were 18 inches tall (45 cm). He could tell, because they were about half as tall as he was. $(36" \div 2 = 18")$

Okay. I, your reader, need some explanation. What's going on? Did the commercial lie?

YnEoS.

What's that mean!

It's a combination of *yes* and *no*. Legally speaking, everything the commercial said was true. On the other hand, the whole thing was one big lie, because it was meant to deceive. Bob and Barbara were very disappointed when they found a hundred trees that were a year-old, rather than trees that were a hundred years old.

It's all a matter of hyphens.

You had better explain, and make it quick. There's a Your Turn to Play coming up on the next page.

You don't know what a hyphen is? It's a short, horizontal bar. It looks like this: -

You use hyphens in writing numbers like *twenty-one* or in words like *daughter-in-law*.

The next is the **en dash**, which is about as long as the letter *n* and looks like: –

Use en dashes for subtraction, $5 - 3 = 2$, or to indicate a span of time, June 2–7.

The longest is the **em dash**, which is about as long as the letter *m* and looks like: —

The em dash has about five different uses. For now, think about it as a giant comma, which makes a big break in a sentence.

Wait! Stop! I know what a hyphen is. I wanted to know about how Fred knew those trees would be small.

I've got four pages in the next (final) chapter of this book to explain all this. Right now, it's . . .

Your Turn to Play

1. What are the tenses of the two verbs?
When Ducky had opened the back of his computer, he discovered a half-eaten sandwich.

2. Proofread this next part of the story. Each paragraph has two errors.

Ducky looked at the sandwich and said "You stupid sandwich"!

Carrying the computer and the sandwich back to the store, his feet hurt. They made him angry.

Back at the store Ducky handed the clerk the half eaten sandwich; he didn't no what to say.

·······ANSWERS·······

1. When Ducky had opened the back of his computer, he discovered a half-eaten sandwich.

Had opened is in the past perfect. It indicates an action that stopped sometime in the past. It was after Ducky had opened his computer that he *discovered*—past tense—the half-eaten sandwich.

2.   Ducky looked at the sandwich and said "You stupid sandwich"!

sandwich!"
The exclamation mark is part of the quoted words.

said, "You
a comma before the open quotes

Carrying the computer and the sandwich back to the store, his feet hurt. They made him angry.

he noticed that his feet hurt.
His feet didn't carry the computer.

What is the antecedent for *they*? Is it his feet or is it the computer with the sandwich in it?

Back at the store Ducky handed the clerk the half eaten sandwich; he didn't no what to say.

know
Spelling error

half-eaten
hyphen needed

Chapter Nineteen
Exceptions

B ob was no longer laughing at Fred. Instead, he asked, "How did you know the trees would be short? Who told you?"

Fred smiled. "The commercial did. It said that they were offering a hundred trees and each tree was a one year old. That's what *100 year-old trees* means.

"If they wanted to advertise that they were selling a bunch of trees that were a hundred years old, they would have written *100-year-old trees.*"

"Oh," said Bob. He thought for a moment and said, "But the advertisement said that they were selling some big trees. I remember them saying *Big tree sale.*"

Fred said, "*Big tree sale* means that they are having a big sale and they are selling trees. It was a big sale. They had 100 trees for sale. If they were selling big trees at their sale, they would have written *big-tree sale.*"

They all climbed back in the car. If Barbara and Bob had known about compound adjectives, they wouldn't have wasted a trip.

Wolfie tried to sit on Fred's lap, but there wasn't enough room. Wolfie had been running among the trees and now smelled like tree sap.

As they headed back to their house, Barbara asked Fred, "Why did you want to be a student at Dubbo School of English? You already seem to know a lot about hyphens. Do you know anything more about those *big tree sale* expressions?"*

Fred answered, "Yes." He was being a little too literal-minded. He missed the *intended meaning* behind the yes-no question.

Barbara said, "Tell us what you know."

Fred began:

---

*When people ask a whole bunch of questions without waiting for an answer to each question, it's often safe to just answer the last question they've asked. After you have answered that question, those people who have asked a flood of questions usually forget their previous questions.

Fred usually listens very carefully to people's questions—the mark of a good teacher—and will answer them all.

In this case, if Fred were to answer (subjunctive mood) Barbara's first question about Fred and the Dubbo School of English, he would have a long story to tell. He would have to start with when he heard in Sunday school about the Board of Missions needing people to teach in foreign lands.

There are two good reasons why Fred will ignore Barbara's first question. First, you, my reader, already know the story. Second, there are only two and half pages left in this book and there is a lot to say about compound adjectives.

Living in the Rule-infested Land
of Compound Adjectives

The first rule is that if you want to take two or more words and place them in front of the noun, you add hyphens.

Example: The land of compound adjectives is infested with rules.

⇒ The rule-infested land

Example: She had nails that were two inches long.

⇒ Her two-inch nails

The second rule, which is an exception to the first rule, is that if the first word ends in –ly, then you do not hyphenate.

Examples: Her highly polished nails

The quickly forgotten song

The third rule, which is an exception to the second rule, is that if the first word ends in –ly and the second word ends in –ing, you do hyphenate.

Examples: The peacefully-sounding voice

The newly-erupting volcano

The fourth rule, which is an exception to the first rule, is do not add a hyphen to a two-word proper noun.

Examples: South American dance

North Dakota corporation

The fifth rule, which is an exception to the fourth rule, is that you do add a hyphen when there are two distinct proper names.

Example: The German-American trading patterns

The San Francisco-Los Angeles-Las Vegas trip

The sixth rule, which is an exception to everything, is the words that have become solid. Solid words are words that are smashed together—no spaces and no hyphens.

Examples: handmade
         lineman
         email
         timesaving

Barbara interrupted, "Wait! How do you tell if a word has become solid?"

Fred said, "It's all a matter of exceptions. *Schoolbook* is solid, but *reference book* isn't. The only way you can tell is to check in a dictionary or on a computer."

Bob said, "All these exceptions! But that's true in any subject. I bet even math is filled with exceptions."

Fred's eyes lit up. "In mathematics, there is only one rule: Don't divide by zero. And there are no exceptions."

They arrived back at Bob and Barbara's house. Everyone got out of the car. Wolfie had a small tree in his mouth.

Index

Index

To learn more about Fred
and the books written about him
visit

FredGauss.com